LIVERPOOL

SEAPORT CITY

LIVERPOOL

SEAPORT CITY

NEIL COSSONS AND MARTIN JENKINS

Ian Allan
PUBLISHING

First published 2011

ISBN 978 0 7110 3421 1

Published by Ian Allan Publishing

An imprint of Ian Allan Publishing Ltd, Hersham, Surrey KT12 4RG.

Printed in England by Ian Allan Printing Ltd, Hersham, Surrey KT12 4RG.

Visit the Ian Allan Publishing website at www.ianallanpublishing.com

Distributed in the United States of America and Canada by BookMasters Distribution Services.

ACKNOWLEDGEMENTS

The authors are indebted to Nigel Bowker, Jonathan Cadwallader, Frederick Maxey, Charles Roberts and Michael Stammers for their invaluable help with compiling the text, scanning pictures and checking captions. John Horne provided the information and text on the gas industry, while Dr Gareth Jenkins provided significant detail relating to aspects of nineteenth- and early twentieth-century Liverpool. Michael Eyre has undertaken invaluable restoration work on many irreplaceable older colour images, which are often badly damaged or faded.

The authors also wish to express their thanks to the following, for providing photographs from their individual collections: John Collingwood; Clive Garner; John Horne; Reverend Stuart Marsh; Frederick Maxey; Freddy O'Connor; Stephen Riley; Glynn Parry; GEC Alsthom Archive; Theatre and Cinema Association; Liverpool Public Record Office.

Some images are reproduced courtesy of the Online Transport Archive (OTA), of which Martin Jenkins is a trustee. Both authors have donated their fees for this book and nearly all photo royalties have been waived, all monies going directly to OTA. Information about this UK registered charity, which was established in 2000 to ensure collections of transport-related slides, photographs and cine-films are secured for posterity, can be obtained from: Online Transport Archive, 8 Aughton Court, Church Road, Upton, Wirral, Cheshire CH49 6JY.

FRONT COVER: Overlooked by Clarence Dock power station, the *Farel* makes her way towards the river through the Trafalgar Lift Bridge on 27 February 1963. *B. D. Pyne, Online Transport Archive*

FRONTISPIECE: Over the years, thousands have admired the many legendary vessels which have berthed at Liverpool. Graced by the recently cleaned trio of waterfront buildings in the background, the Royal Yacht *Britannia* paid a visit in 1977 during the Queen's Silver Jubilee celebrations. *J. G. Parkinson, Online Transport Archive*

MIX
Paper from responsible sources
FSC® C014615
FSC
www.fsc.org

CONTENTS

INTRODUCTION 7

I   THE DOCKS 12

II   TRANSPORT 62

III   INDUSTRY 86

IV   ARCHITECTURE AND HOUSING 92

V   THE COMMERCIAL CITY 95

VI   THE CIVIC CITY 105

VII   THE CULTURAL CITY 108

VIII   URBAN DEVELOPMENT 113

IX   WELFARE AND MEDICAL PROVISION 129

X   GAS AND ELECTRICITY 133

XI   RELIGION AND CHURCHES 136

XII   THE PRESS 143

XIII   LAW AND ORDER 144

XIV   LOCAL COMMERCE 146

XV   ENTERTAINMENT AND CULTURE 149

XVI   PUBS 154

XVII   SPORT 157

SELECT BIBLIOGRAPHY 159

INTRODUCTION

Liverpool is one of the great cities of the world. Indeed, it was recognised as a 'world city' long before the term became common currency. Throughout its history, it is the distinctiveness and exceptionalism of Liverpool that has constantly been remarked upon. It has always has been a city like no other; on the edge of one world, looking out towards another.

In these descriptions of Liverpool, three themes recur: the extraordinary wealth and dynamism of the burgeoning seaport; the reflection of that wealth in its great buildings and spectacular cityscape; and the huge contrast between mercantile affluence and the condition of the Liverpool poor. But there is, of course, a fourth theme that underscores all of these: Liverpool's people, the root of the city's pride and its personality, and sometimes of its problems.

Liverpool is a city where superlatives have always been inadequate. In 1907, when it celebrated the 700th anniversary of its charter, Liverpool proudly proclaimed itself the 'second city of empire ... There is no part of the globe, however remote, whose natives may not be met on the Liverpool landing stage, and there is no territory so distant whose products do not pass ... through the docks and warehouses of Liverpool.'

Half a century earlier, Thomas Baines in his *History of the Commerce and Town of Liverpool* had asserted that, 'the commerce of Liverpool extends to every port of any importance in every quarter of the globe ... and fully equals, if it does not surpass, that of London and New York,' while a French visitor in 1860 noted that the 'spectacle of Liverpool docks is one of the greatest in the world'.

Generations of Liverpudlians have liked to think of themselves as part of a global community. And there was truth in that self-image; they had more in common with the people of other great port cities like Hamburg or Marseilles than with, say, the hinterland of industrial Lancashire. It's an abiding part of the Liverpool myth that the city is bigger and better than all the rest. But, of course, the more accurate comparison would be with New York. The symbiotic relationship between the two cities can still be seen in the Liverpool of today, with a waterfront caricatured as 'Manhattan on Mersey'.

The city's trading connections go back much further, initially via links to Ireland and the western seaboard of Europe. They extended from the early 1700s onwards through the notorious triangular trade, in which ships left Liverpool for Africa, bartering goods for slaves that they took to Caribbean and North American colonies to exchange for tropical cargoes such as sugar, tobacco, coffee, dyewoods and cotton. As the monopolistic influence of the Royal Africa Company declined, so Liverpool's interests grew. In 1730, there were 15 slave traders in Liverpool; by 1753, there were over a hundred. Between 1700 and the outlawing of slavery in Britain and her dominions under the 1807 Act of Parliament, Liverpool's slave traders are thought to have undertaken 5,000 passages with human cargo across the Atlantic.

The trade also fuelled Liverpool's iron, gunsmithery, hardware and drapery industries, while Manchester's textile merchants similarly benefited. The debate about the slave trade's abolition in the late 18th century therefore resulted in apocalyptic anxieties about economic ruin and 'grass in the streets', but Liverpool's mercantile class would be astute and resilient enough to exploit other business opportunities.

The growing strength of the industrial Midlands and the expanding output from Lancashire's cotton towns gave Liverpool its next boost. Links first by canal and later by rail made the city the leading export port of Britain – and the largest in Europe – by the mid-19th century. The connections were by now predominantly with the United States. By mid-century, New York was the principal destination for ships leaving Liverpool; the second was New Orleans, as the cotton importer's gateway to the Mississippi and Missouri. By 1850, Liverpool's export trade was double that of London and half that of the nation as a whole. More overseas trade was based in Liverpool than in any other city. By 1873, the Liverpool-based Pacific Steam Navigation Company was said to be the largest shipping company in the world and the city's merchants had secured the largest share of West African trade.

Between 1860 and 1900, out of the 5.5 million people who left Europe for life in the New World some 4.75 million had departed from Liverpool. But many stayed, of course, adding to the diversity of a cultural mix already the subject of comment and controversy. Most numerous were the Irish, especially after the famine years of the 1840s. Many passed through Liverpool on their way elsewhere, but those who stayed were to form the largest Catholic community in Britain. It was in part their presence and its perceived threat that consolidated Liverpool's Protestant hegemony, resulting in unbroken political control exercised over the city by essentially Protestant and Tory business interests from 1842 to 1955. However, by now the city that Lord Erskine had described, in 1791, as 'fit to be the capital of any empire in the world' was an even more diverse and extraordinary place.

This 'exceptionalism' – the term generally used to describe Liverpool's uniquely unusual situation – permeates every aspect of the city's history. Half-measures were as rarely used in describing the darker side of the city as in celebrating its glories. In a contemporary quote Liverpool was a city where 'poverty was more desperate, housing more squalid, the state of public health more shocking and social distinctions more cruel' than any other. In 1885, the Unitarian minister and social reformer, Richard Acland Armstrong (1843-1905) saw this poverty in vivid relief:

> 'I came to Liverpool a stranger ... knowing only that I was about to take up my residence in the second city of the mightiest Empire the world has ever seen. I admired its public buildings, its vast docks, its stately shipping, its splendid shops, its lovely parks ... But ... I was appalled

Bibby Street, Old Swan, 8 June 1969. *Cedric Greenwood*

by one aspect of things here … The contiguity of immense wealth and abysmal poverty forced itself upon my notice. The hordes of the ragged and the wretched surged up from their native quarters and covered the noblest streets like a flood. Men and women in the cruellest grip of poverty, like children with shoeless feet, bodies pinched and faces in which the pure light of childhood had been quenched, swarmed on the very pavements that fronted the most brilliant shops; and the superb carriages of the rich, with their freights of refined and elegant ladies, threaded their way among sections of the population so miserable and squalid that my heart ached at the sight of them. I had seen wealth. I had seen poverty. But never before had I seen the two so jammed together.'

The city of today dates mainly from the last 200 years. Although Liverpool enjoyed rapid and unprecedented growth from the early 18th century, such was the accelerated rate of subsequent developments that they have largely obscured what went before. From the completion of the world's first enclosed wet dock, in 1715, the city's expansion soon confirmed its already strong position as gateway to Ireland and, increasingly, to North America and the wider world. Liverpool was, above all, the city that benefited from imperial aspirations and was able to exploit it; an Atlantic city, a fulcrum between the Old World and the New. Just as today, when Britain's trade is predominantly with her European partners, it is the ports of the Southeast of England that enjoy most geographical advantages.

Despite this, Liverpool still handles huge tonnages of container traffic through its Seaforth terminal, largely invisible to most people, with a labour force that is only a fraction of its former days. As the most centrally positioned deep-sea port in Britain, Liverpool is ideally situated to serve the northern half of the country. It typically offers savings in excess of £150 and (on an environmental rather than economic level) 0.5 tons of carbon dioxide per container compared to those entering through one of the southern ports and delivering to their final destination by truck. In the past few years, Liverpool has already seen a 15 per cent increase in the number of containers delivered to the Northwest, despite an overall 20 per cent downturn in container traffic in the United Kingdom as a whole.

Boundary Street / Luton Street, 14 June 1964. *Cedric Greenwood*

It has been this move away from the old dockland areas and the decline in traditional financial and ship-owning interests that, despite the devastating effects of the Luftwaffe in World War 2, has made modern Liverpool such an astounding urban environment. The character of Liverpool has also survived due to an absence of many of the redevelopment pressures and overambitious planning interventions that irrevocably altered so many British cities in the post-war years. What remains is a city whose heroic stature is evident in every part of its history.

The innovation so synonymous with Liverpool can also be seen in its transport history. Great skill and perseverance were shown by successive generations of dock engineers, who designed and built ever more docks, warehouses and transit sheds for the increasing tonnage that passed through the port. Especially notable today are the works of Jesse Hartley (1780-1860), the world's first fulltime professional dock engineer, who over a period of nearly forty years transformed Liverpool's docks by a programme of continuous expansion and improvement.

Rail transport as we know it also has its origins in the Liverpool & Manchester Railway of 1830, the world's first passenger-carrying steam railway which, in its design and operation, was hugely influential on the development of the railways as a transport system. The Mersey Railway of 1886, passing under the river to Birkenhead, and the Liverpool Overhead Railway of 1893, both with their American-style rolling stock, were innovative responses to specialised local needs. Between 1898-1944, Liverpool Corporation also built one of the country's finest electric tram systems, with spaciously planned suburbs developed around its central tramway reservations.

Further innovation is seen in the fight to eradicate poverty and disease. The country's first Medical Officer of Health, City Engineer and Water Engineer were all appointed in Liverpool during the 1840s. Of necessity, the city was to become a leader in the provision of social housing, firstly to eliminate the appalling cellar dwellings, and then the courts and later sub-standard terraced housing. This process started in 1869; later, especially in the interwar years, Liverpool became well-known for the design and quality of its council houses.

Liverpool University also pioneered tropical medicine and civic planning, both directly related not only to the needs of the city itself but to those of the wider world. The work of architects who trained in Liverpool, at one of the first university-based schools of architecture, also

Chadwick Street, 14 June 1964. *Cedric Greenwood*

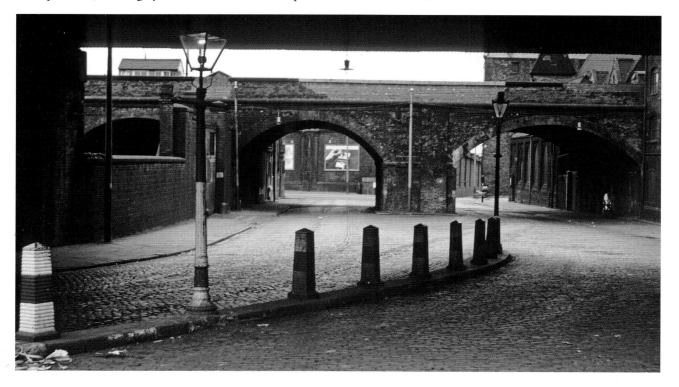

had a strong influence on the character of the city. Links with American architectural style are reflected in the design of many Liverpool buildings, with steel-framing and fire-proofing appearing early in the 20th century.

Between 1700 and 1801 (the time of the first census), the population rose from approximately 5,000 to 77,653, a 15-fold increase – a higher average percentage rise per decade than throughout the 19th century. The mortality rate was also very high, most of the population increase being due to inward migration. By 1900, the population had grown to 684,958, nearly nine times that of a century earlier, with the highest rate of growth in the first 40 years of the intervening period.

By then numbers were beginning to fall in the central areas, as people were rehoused in rapidly growing suburbs. The peak was recorded in the 1931 census as 855,688. Since then there has been a steady decline, so that by 2001 there were 439,473 people living in the city, a fall of some 50 per cent. The historian and social reformer Margaret Simey (1906-2004) encapsulated

TOP: Upper Parliament Street, May 1971.

RIGHT: Grassendale Park entrance, 15 April 1978. *Cedric Greenwood*

Liverpool's dilemma in a nutshell when she noted ruefully in 1996 how it 'was a port, a great port, and ominously nothing but a port'. At the dawn of the new century, despite the efforts of government and numerous financial incentives, Liverpool still headed the list of the ten most deprived local authorities in England.

But by then the city's fortunes were showing positive signs of revival. Regeneration of the waterfront, which had begun in the 1980s at Albert Dock, has continued both north and south of the Pier Head into the central business district and the Ropewalk area. Reflecting trends in other disadvantaged cities – especially declining port cities – throughout the world, redundant buildings that a generation earlier had been regarded as obsolete were suddenly seen as assets when converted into apartments. The main engine of change was a combination of Liverpool's spectacular setting, its proliferation of redeveloped warehouses and office buildings and the willingness of well-heeled young professionals to live close to cultural, entertainment, nightlife and retail centres.

As a result, in the last twenty years population in the central areas has grown for the first time in a century. New museums and galleries, the restoration of St George's Hall, the opening of Liverpool One – one of Europe's largest new retail developments – new cafés, restaurants and hotels have brought back something of the vitality of former years. Listing by UNESCO as a World Heritage Site in 2004, based on the city's former mercantile might, brought international recognition of Liverpool's distinctiveness. So too did designation as European Capital of Culture 2008, coinciding with the 800th anniversary of its charter. Ironically, it was the geopolitical pull of Europe – which had in part marginalised Liverpool as a port – that led the European Union to award the city its highest category of grant funding, reserved for communities where the per capita GDP was below 75 per cent of the EU average.

For some, this new service-based economy has eroded Liverpool's distinctive character, discarding its former mercantile and maritime environment in favour of a new form of urban habitat. An alternative view might question what other options are on offer and stress that the benefits of regeneration through conservation, 'using reminders of Britain's industrial heyday, retaining their character and heritage while redefining their functions,' will attract inward investment to both expand and diversify the city's still fragile economy.

Another view, reflecting that phlegmatic Liverpudlian indifference to any news, good or bad, might be that we've seen it all before and that there have been any number of revivals, none of them to any lasting benefit. The Beatles, undoubtedly Liverpool's most famous export in the post-war years, and the Mersey Beat are frequently cited in this context. Long gone are the days when the American beat poet Allen Ginsberg (1926-97) saw Liverpool as 'the centre of the consciousness of the human universe'. The rejoinders from those gritty scousers who then – as now – saw themselves as guardians of all that was special and much that was perverse in Liverpool's character are not recorded. Ken Dodd, the most enduring of a long sequence of Merseyside comics, perhaps captured most acutely the spirit of the city when he said, 'You have to be a comedian to live here.'

Liverpool, like so many great historic cities, has been through cycles of growth, decline and now renaissance. In Liverpool's case the rise was dazzling and dramatic and the decline calamitous, while today's renaissance – although still fragile in economic terms – has restored a spirit of pride and optimism to a city battered by generations of hardship and constant change. In the robustness of its urban environment, Liverpool is still a city with immense depth of character.

In this book we chart Liverpool's fortunes, from the peak of its prosperity and global influence in the mid-19th century down to today. It is a period that coincides with the rise of photography, thus it is through public and private photographic archives that Liverpool's multiplicity of faces is seen. A number of the scenes will be familiar, but we hope that most of the illustrations themselves are not. Many have never been published and, whenever possible, colour images have been selected, some nearly 60 years old.

In order to present Liverpool's role as a great seaport in a wider context and to fully understand its extraordinary character, we look not only at the history of the docks, shipping, public transport and industry, but at the wider urban environment with its eclectic mix of commercial, residential, civic and religious buildings. The emphasis on colour illustrations also gives us the opportunity to present often surprising views of Liverpool. What we hope in part to reveal is the tough reality of a great port city photographed during some of the most challenging years of its history.

I   THE DOCKS

If the Mersey is the life blood of Liverpool, then the docks and the miles of quays were for many years its veins and arteries. The Industrial Revolution, the establishment of worldwide trading links and the development of the dock system all contributed to Liverpool's place as the 'second port of empire' and Europe's foremost transatlantic port.

The story of the docks began in the latter part of the 17th century when a number of merchants, some of whom had relocated following the Great Fire of London, financed construction of a berth where vessels would be safe from the vagaries of the turbulent river, with its 31-foot tidal range, unstable sandbanks, strong westerly winds and unpredictable currents.

The world's first commercial deep-water wet dock was designed by Thomas Steers. As Liverpool's first Dock Master and Water Bailiff, he transformed a former tidal pool into a dock capable of accommodating 100 vessels in an area of water protected behind floodgates. Leaving the river, ships manoeuvred under sail into a tidal basin from where they were taken to the open quaysides. Opened on 31 August 1715, New Dock became the focus for a rapidly developing community. Recent excavations have revealed the solidity and complexity of its construction.

Dutch-born Steers, who later became Lord Mayor of Liverpool, was later involved in the 1753 construction of Salthouse Dock, a pier and positioning marker buoys in the river's main channel. He also designed a church, a theatre and early merchant housing.

Subsequent dock expansion in the late 18th century was presided over by William Hutchinson, Henry Berry and Thomas Morris. Faced by hilly terrain to the east of the river, these and most subsequent docks were built on land reclaimed from the river's margins. Over the years and well into the 20th century, many of the docks were later reconstructed or enlarged, while others like George's Dock (1771) were subsequently infilled. The ruthless drive to construct quay space led to the disappearance of the natural coastline and many earlier river-based industries such as shipbuilding, which had vanished by 1898.

Dock construction led to the first major wave of mass migration into Liverpool, increasing the population to 75,000 by 1800. By then, the 4,000 vessels using the docks accounted for one sixth of all English tonnage and had provided Customs and Excise with £680,000. Many merchants and ship owners derived their wealth mostly from the notorious triangular trade whereby a ship left Liverpool with goods for Africa, which were exchanged for slaves to be taken to the New World. Vessels completed the triangle by returning to port laden with coffee, cotton, sugar, tobacco and rum. Anti-abolitionists argued that ending the slave trade would ruin Liverpool, but once it became illegal the merchants developed new markets, for example in the Far East, while salt was despatched to the American colonies and coal to the West Indies.

To discourage pilferage, Prince's Dock (opened 1821) lay behind a protective wall. Designed by John Foster Senior in conjunction with John Rennie, it took ten years to build. Foster's successor was the Yorkshire-born bridge builder and engineer Jesse Hartley, who was dock surveyor from 1824 to 1860. His docks, basins, quays and warehouses made a lasting impact on the Liverpool waterfront and, despite having no prior experience of dock construction, he proved to be an innovative genius. Rough in attitude and manner, he spent wisely, achieved the highest standards, understood man-management and possessed an infinite grasp of detail coupled with organisational flair. He also built to last, with materials such as Scottish granite.

Hartley also exercised a steely determination to exclude all other parties from the Dock Estate. Most of his early designs followed the shape and pattern established at Prince's, but he rose to the challenge as wooden ships gave way to iron and sails to ever bigger steamships. When Hartley's Albert Dock opened in 1846, it was the world's first secure dock to be enclosed by fireproof warehouses. Next came a massive expansion with a clutch of five interconnected docks opening in 1848, one of which, Stanley, lay on the landward side of the dock road and was connected to the Leeds & Liverpool Canal. Responding to pressure from HM Customs to deter intruders, Hartley enclosed much of the Dock Estate behind substantial walls featuring castellated entrances and ornate police lodges. He also invested in hydraulic power.

Although Jesse Hartley provided Liverpool with a modern dock system, it was men like John Bramley-Moore who, as Chairman of the Dock Committee, raised and provided the money. In 1858, administrative control of the Dock Estate passed from the town council and the Dock Ratepayers to the Mersey Docks & Harbour Board (MD&HB), who also controlled the Birkenhead Docks. From its inception, the MD&HB employed highly-paid engineers and architects, men with verve, vision and

ingenuity. Ongoing problems included delays at river entrances caused by low water and the need to constantly dredge the principal channels in Liverpool Bay. When Hartley died in 1860 he was succeeded by his son, J. B. Hartley, who, unlike his father, was adept at dealing with local and national politicians.

When G. F. Lyster became Dock Engineer in 1861, some 21,000 vessels used the port; the dock wall extended for six miles, with 256 acres of enclosed water and some 18 miles of quays. It was Lyster (and later his son) who supervised construction of the larger docks, built mostly in the neighbouring borough of Bootle. To ensure a quicker turnaround, they had improved entrances, larger stretches of water and massive dockside facilities capable of accommodating the grandest liners and the biggest cargo ships. By the time this period of expansion had ended, with completion of the 56-acre Gladstone Dock complex in 1927, total tonnage exceeded 20 million.

To sustain their economic viability, the MD&HB pursued a programme of upgrading older docks, some of which were adapted and modified though others were redesigned and, in some cases, rebuilt. Where appropriate, newer docks were also modernised or altered to provide facilities for the import/export of different commodities. There was also an ongoing commitment to improving the troublesome river entrances.

During World War 2, the entire system worked to capacity. Many ships were destroyed or incapacitated either in the river or at the quaysides. Ninety acres of

Under the watchful eye of the Dock Master, Ellerman & Papayanni Lines' *Venetian* (1947, 3578 gross register tonnage) enters Gladstone Lock with the Alexandra Towing Company tug *Nelson* (1935, 192 grt). *G. H. Hesketh*

warehouses and transit sheds were wiped out and another 90 acres badly damaged. Repairs were executed swiftly and in the post-war period new sheds and quayside cranes were installed. In 1954 some 18,000 vessels used the port, which then handled over 26 million tons of cargo.

Some claim the port's downturn began in the 1960s, but in reality economic decline had started decades earlier; shock waves had been felt before World War 1, when White Star transferred its premier transatlantic passenger crossings to Southampton. After World War 2, often bitter industrial relations and strikes led the shipping lines to desert Liverpool. With many of the older docks now an increasing financial liability, all the south docks were closed in 1972. A year later, an entirely new type of dock – Royal Seaforth, which embraced the latest, most cost-effective technology – was opened on land reclaimed from the river. Shortly after, the bankrupt MD&HB was succeeded by the Mersey Dock & Harbour Company. Since 1984, Royal Seaforth has been at the heart of a self-contained Freeport and is currently owned by Peel Holdings Ltd.

Today, some of the former south docks form part of a World Heritage site; some have been in-filled and some converted for other uses, housing new buildings that include Liverpool *Echo Arena*, HMS *Eaglet* and a Revenue & Customs Building.

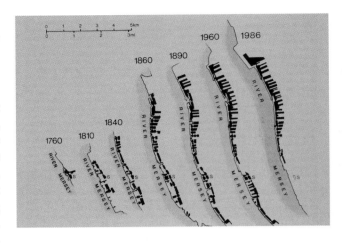

ABOVE: These maps show the development of the Dock Estate from 1760 to 1960.

BELOW: Owned and operated by the London & North Western Railway (L&NWR), the Port of Garston Docks first became part of the City of Liverpool in 1902. Served directly by rail, Old Dock (opened 1853), North (1875) and Stalbridge (1909) were interlinked and equipped for bunkering and exporting coal, especially to Ireland. Major imports included bananas, chemicals, metal ores and timber. These docks (28½ acres) remain open but the much-reduced rail links have been mothballed. On 14 March 1977, the Ramsey Steamship Company's *Ben Veg* (launched 1965, 346 grt) was in Old Dock and two of the original four coal tips on the east quay had been removed. *Nigel Bowker*

BELOW: The most southerly of the MD&HB docks was Herculaneum (opened 1866, 13 acres expanded from the original ten). Visible in the September 1968 are Cammell Laird's shipyard across the river, the entrance into Harrington Dock (right), the clock tower on East Toxteth's shed, the *Hemsley 1* (left) and the MD&HB crane *Titan* (right). Still extant and built into rock under Grafton Street (foreground) are 60 casemates designed to store inflammable materials. Dangerous fuels not allowed into the docks were discharged through pipes from vessels anchored at jetties directly into the nearby Dingle Tank Farm. These refined fuels then left by barge, ship, road or rail. At this time, the coastal motor tanker *Herbert D* (1953, 890 grt) was owned by Celtic Coasters of Cork. Designed by Jesse Hartley and built on the site of a copper-works and a famous pottery, the complex included graving docks for ship repair work, coal bunkering facilities and a yard to repair and maintain buoys. After closure, 'Herky' was later in-filled to provide access to the 1984 International Garden Festival. Today, the site is occupied by a mix of offices and apartments. *Nigel Bowker*

LEFT: The interlinked Harrington (built 1883) and Toxteth (1888) Docks were created by G. F. Lyster from three older tidal basins. Both had the world's first double-storey transit sheds where each storey worked independently, the lower using ship and quayside equipment while the upper had hydraulically-powered, roof-mounted cranes. For many years, the principal imports were cocoa, palm oil, groundnuts and hardwoods. This 1970 view of Harrington was taken looking south towards the passage into Herculaneum, the river entrance and Dingle Tank Farm (background). The *Amarna* (launched 1949, 3,422 GRT) belonged to the Liverpool shipping line Moss Hutchinson, while the Spanish vessel *Nova Hermosa* (1958, 971 grt) was under charter for use on the Trafume Line service to Spain. *Nigel Bowker*

BOTTOM: Awaiting disposal in Toxteth (11 acres) in 1971 are the Ellerman Line's *Catanian* (1958, 1,407 grt) and *Malatian* (1958, 1,420 grt), while the Mossgiel Steamship Company's *Cortian* (1962, 537 grt) has been chartered by Ellerman. *Nigel Bowker*

TOP: Jesse Hartley's first dock was Brunswick (opened 1832, 12 acres). Built on the site of a tidal flourmill and millpond, it was designed for the timber trade and provided with two graving docks. When the timber trade migrated to the north end, Brunswick handled coal, meat, heavy machinery and grain. In the early 1900s, its capacity was increased to 17 acres when an impressive new river entrance gave access to most of the south docks. In 1936, a concrete grain silo was built at the northeast end. *A. Collingwood*

MIDDLE: Seen in November 1970, the Royal Mail Line's *Lombardy* (1958, 8,015 grt) is alongside the silo. To the left is the older, brick-built silo of 1906. *Nigel Bowker*

BOTTOM: In 1840, the river entrance to the basin serving the small Union Dock was fitted with gates and named Coburg (after the Saxe-Coburg family). In 1858, Coburg and Union were combined to create a new east-west seven-acre dock with new transit sheds, passages into the docks on either side and a wide river entrance allowing it to be used by Cunard's new liners, among others. In 1906, a grain silo was built at the eastern end. This view of the pneumatic grain elevators which transferred the grain from ship to silo dates from 1933. *A. Collingwood*

TOP: For some years, the MD&HB had workshops at Coburg. Seen in dock in the late 1950s, alongside the Isle of Man Steam Packet Co freighter *Peveril* (built 1929, 798 grt), are *C8* and *C20*, two MD&HB light floats assigned to the Crosby Channel (one of the most important channels in approaching the port), and the former lightship *Star* (1885, 195 net register tonnage). After being reduced to a sand barge, she was only broken up in 1990. Astern of *C20* was *Mersey No 40*, a grab hopper dredger (1957, 1,968 grt) moored alongside the ICI Weaver packet *Frances Poole*. *G. H. Hesketh*

MIDDLE AND BOTTOM: King's and Queen's Docks were designed by Thomas Morris. The latter six-acre north-south dock (opened 1796), named after Queen Charlotte Sophia, was the base for Liverpool's whaling fleet. Between 1810 and 1816, it was redesigned for the timber trade. In 1858, it was altered when the new Coburg Dock was opened and finally, between 1898 and 1906, it was transformed into a 21-acre complex with a main dock and two east-west branches flanking a graving dock. The first view, taken on 26 February 1966, shows MacAndrew and Co's *Verdaguer* (1958, 2,049 grt) berthed at the north quay of Branch Dock No 2, while the second view, taken in March 1971, shows the *Kaduna* (1956, 5,599 grt) berthed alongside the transit sheds with their roof-mounted cranes in Branch Dock No 1. Although owned by the Henderson Line of Glasgow, the *Kaduna* was operating on an Elder Dempster West African service. Visible in the background is the African Oil Mills building on Chaloner Street. *Ian Holt, Nigel Bowker*

RIGHT: The seven-acre north-south King's Dock (1785-88) catered at first for the lucrative North American tobacco trade, with bonded warehouses and a colossal tobacco pipe with a 100-foot stem and a massive bowl to consume damaged tobacco. Most of the site was swept away during the construction of Wapping Dock (1858), after which King's was reduced in size and the river entrance serving King's and Queen's fitted with double gates to create additional water space. When this entrance closed in 1906, Wapping and King's effectively became a single body of water, the latter now comprising two east-west docks with an overall water space of seven acres. Overlooked by the five-storey Wapping warehouse and flanked by transit sheds with roof-mounted cranes, the Greek vessel *Elona* (1925, 4,011 grt) is seen in Dock No 1 in 1970. *Nigel Bowker*

BELOW: The opening of Wapping Basin and Wapping Dock in 1858 linked the previously unconnected parts of the south docks, increased quay space and reduced the number of troublesome river entrances. It was used mainly by ships in transit, though smaller coasters also used the Wapping berths. The Hartley warehouse (opened 1856) had massive vaults and five storeys rising from the quayside. Parts were bombed during World War 2, with masonry damaging the adjacent Overhead Railway. After serving as a bonded liquor store until 1988, the war-damaged section was torn down and the remainder converted into apartments. *J. G. Parkinson, Online Transport Archive*

LEFT: The privately owned two-acre Duke's Dock (opened 1773) was acquired by the MD&HB in 1899. Built and named after the third Duke of Bridgewater, goods were brought here from the Manchester area in Mersey 'flats' (the distinctive local barges) via the Bridgewater Canal. The dock eventually had over 160 buildings, including an eight-storey warehouse (1783) and a Venetian-style, six-storey grain warehouse (1811). Now closed to the river, only a section of the original dock wall is visible. *Commercial postcard, courtesy of John Horne*

BELOW: South (later Salthouse) Dock (1753) was a major engineering achievement taking nineteen years to build out into the river and protected behind massive walls. Following completion of Albert Dock, it became part of a cost-saving 'one-way system' whereby sailing ships offloaded in Albert before reloading in Salthouse with cargo assembled in single-storey granite-built transit sheds. Awaiting scrap in 1926 is HMS *Eaglet*, one of many pensioned-off naval vessels which once served as training ships for the Royal and Merchant Navies. Launched in 1804 as HMS *Eagle*, she came to the Mersey in 1862 and was renamed in 1918. In the background is the Custom House. *H. N. Cooper, John Collingwood collection*

ABOVE: The Albert Dock complex stands today as a brooding memorial to the genius of its designer, Jesse Hartley. During its seven-year construction at a cost of £722,000, several shipbuilding yards ceased trading as the Canning and Salthouse Docks were drained of water. Condemned by contemporary critics as 'monstrous' and 'ugly', Liverpool's first enclosed dock, with its secure brick and iron warehouse stacks, was opened by Prince Albert in 1846. Berthed on the east side in 1949 are the MD&HB's *Galatea* (1906, 588 grt), the Light Float *Q11* (black), a starboard marker for Queen's Channel and the *North West* (red and white stripes). *G. H. Hesketh*

RIGHT: Scores of naval vessels were repaired in the two veteran graving docks during World War 2, although No 1 was eventually put out of action. Seen in 1949, Liverpool Pilot Cutter No 4 (launched 1937, 579 GRT) William M. Clarke is in the company of two light floats (or boat beacons), undergoing final inspection before returning to Liverpool Bay. Today, as part of the Maritime Museum, Graving Dock No 1 is home to the pilot cutter *Edmund Gardner* and No 2 to the schooner *De Wadden. G. H. Hesketh*

BELOW: Today, the area in and around Canning Dock is of major historical importance. In 1737, Steers improved access to New Dock by excavating an outer tidal basin and building three graving docks on its northwest side (left). When the basin was fitted with watertight gates in 1813, it was named after the Liverpool MP George Canning. Seen in 1949, the dumb barge (i.e. without sail or rigging) *Lonsdale* (1908) is offloading river-dredged sand at a south-side berth assigned to Richard Abel & Sons. Contemporary cargoes included gravel, stone and, occasionally, refrigerated fruit. Also in dock are a Belfast Steamship Company vessel, the steam coaster *Talacre* (1917, 301 grt), owned by the National Coal Board, and the static club ship *Landfall* (built by Hawthorn Leslie), then owned by the Honourable Company of Master Mariners. Although a key part of the National Historic Ships Collection, this World War 2 tank landing craft is in a semi-derelict condition. Before construction of the buildings in the background, Canning was linked with George's Dock to the north. *G. H. Hesketh*

LEFT: In the late 1880s, the horse buses and trams congregating at the Pier Head were privately owned; the floating roadway already lay in the cut behind the rank of horse-drawn cabs, The Overhead Railway did not exist and George's Dock still handled deliveries of fruit and vegetables. Of the background buildings, only Our Lady and St Nicholas (patron saint of seafarers) churches still survive. Until the latter part of the 18th century, the waterline had been in front of St Nicholas' Church. Like Salthouse, George's Dock (1771-1900) was built out into the river's margins. Today, most of this former dock is occupied by the great waterfront buildings. Although a religious site for centuries, the oldest part of the church at this time was its 120-foot tower capped with a 60-foot buttressed lantern spire (1811-1815). During World War 2, most of the church was damaged but subsequently rebuilt. Bull baiting once took place in the grounds here, and guns were positioned to deter invasion. It is claimed a peal from the church bells caused an earlier tower to collapse, killing some visiting children. Later, the Prince's pub (left) was demolished to make way for an entrance to the Mersey Tunnel; the offices of the local shipping line T&J Harrison were bombed in 1941 and the original Tower Building (1852) replaced by the present block in 1910. *F. Frith – courtesy of Martin Jenkins, David Packer and Jerome McWatt, Online Transport Archive*

ABOVE: By 26 August 1904, the Overhead Railway had been running for ten years and the MD&HB headquarters was under construction. The exposed sections of George's Dock would later become the cellars of the Cunard and Liver Buildings. Along the waterfront from left to right are the Chester and Ellesmere Basin (early 1780s, enlarged 1818, closed 1920s), George's Baths (1829-1906) and the various passenger bridges to the landing stage. The original George's Landing Stage (ferry boats, 1847-1874) and Prince's Landing Stage (liners and other passenger ships, 1857-1896) were soon too small. George's was replaced by a new structure in 1875, which in turn was linked in 1896 to a new Prince's Stage. Last extended in 1922, this was the world's longest floating landing stage (at 2,533 feet x 80 feet), until replaced by a much smaller structure in the 1970s. *Liverpool City Engineers, Martin Jenkins collection*

RIGHT: Contrasting with the skyline of sailing ships in Prince's Dock, the White Star Line's *Majestic* (1890, 9,881 grt) is seen at Prince's Landing Stage in 1898. Visible alongside is a tender and, in the distance, the Prince's Dockmaster's office and the hydraulic engine house where a bridge leading into the half-tide dock was raised. The *Majestic* was broken up in Morecambe Bay in 1914.
F. Frith, Martin Jenkins, David Packer and Jerome McWatt, Online Transport Archive

BELOW: By the time this panorama was taken in 1921, all three waterfront buildings had been completed and the tram layout consisted of three loops. Connecting George's Pier Head to Prince's Landing Stage was the 550-foot floating roadway. Designed by G. F. Lyster, it rested on pontoons which rose and fell with the tide and gave vehicle access to the stage – including the cross-river luggage boats, the last of which operated in 1947. The distinctive granite obelisk was erected in 1916 as a memorial to the heroes of the marine engine room on the *Titanic*.
Clive Garner collection

In its heyday the landing stage was used by millions, including royalty, celebrities, troops and immigrants. Mixing with day-trippers boarding a Liverpool and North Wales steamer on this sunny day are passengers disembarking from an Isle of Man Steam Packet Company vessel. The high level gangway (right) moved on rails, so that it could be positioned to provide additional access to larger liners. The decking rested on 200 wrought-iron pontoons which moved vertically and horizontally to accommodate the tidal movements of the river. The stage was secured to the river wall by a combination of booms, mooring chains and hinged passenger bridges. During stormy weather, the whole flexible structure groaned and creaked alarmingly as it bucked and swayed with the current. *A. S. Clayton collection, Online Transport Archive*

BELOW: Among the shipping lines established in Liverpool were Anchor, Bibby, Blue Funnel, Booth, Canadian Pacific, Harrison, White Star and, of course, Cunard. Representing generations of legendary liners to grace the stage is this classic study of the Cunarder *Franconia* (launched 1923, 20,341 GRT), taken in the Coronation year of 1953. Having transported 150,000 troops during World War 2 and served as the floating headquarters for the Yalta Conference, her final crossing from New York to Liverpool was in 1956. *J. B. C. McCann, Online Transport Archive*

RIGHT: Ferries have crossed the Mersey since the 13th century. For many years, Birkenhead Corporation maintained its frequent Woodside service with a quintet of locally built, coal-fired steamers (1925-1933). In 1960, we see the *Claughton* (launched 1930, 487 grt) leaving George's Landing while the *Royal Daffodil II* (1958, 609 grt), the last three-decker acquired by Wallasey Corporation, heads for Seacombe. High-capacity vessels were needed when, at one point, 44 per cent of the town's population were employed in Liverpool and also for the once-popular New Brighton service which closed in 1971. *Neil Cossons*

RIGHT: Jesse Hartley's original six-acre east-west Waterloo Dock (opened 1834) underwent a major reconfiguration by G. F. Lyster between 1863-1868, after which the nine-acre site comprised two north-south branch docks (East and West Waterloo) with warehouses for imported grain. For many years, access was from Trafalgar to the north and Prince's Half Tide Dock to the south, the latter closed when the West Waterloo river entrance opened in 1949. The Clyde Shipping Company passenger cargo steamer *Tuskar* is seen working the Wexford service in the entrance lock on 27 February 1965. This entrance closed in 1988, with the end of commercial activity at Waterloo Dock. *B. D. Pyne, Online Transport Archive*

BELOW: In their latter days, the central block of docks from Prince's to Nelson were used by smaller vessels engaged in coastwise and short sea trades. Most are now redundant. Originally the principal dock for the North Atlantic trade, with transit sheds on its east and west quays, Prince's (opened 1821) was adapted several times for different types of traffic. Access was improved when the tidal basin at the north end was transformed into a half-tide dock with triple river entrance in 1868. Eventually too shallow and too confined for the new breed of liners, it became a base for expensive imports such as coffee and spices. Then, in the 20th century, it was modernised for the Irish passenger and freight trade. In 1961, we see the Coast Line's *Irish Coast* (launched 1952, 3,824 grt) berthed at its eastern quay, covering for a British and Irish (B&I) Steam Packet Company vessel on its Dublin service, while at the western quay are the two-funnel Belfast Steamship Company vessels *Ulster Monarch* (launched 1929, 3,802 grt) and *Ulster Premier* (1955, 979 grt). Seen in the background of West Waterloo Dock is the MD&HB grab hopper dredger *Mersey No 40* (1957, 1,968 grt) and, just off the river entrance, the Clyde Shipping Company's cargo steamer *Rockabill* (1931, 1,445 grt), which regularly brought cattle 'on the hoof' to the lairage at Woodside. After Prince's Dock closed in 1981, it was partly in-filled and is home today to offices and hotels. *Tom Parkinson, Online Transport Archive*

ABOVE: The history of the Hartley docks – Victoria, Trafalgar and Clarence – are interlinked. Named after the Duke of Clarence (later William IV), the latter was opened in 1830 with its half-tide and graving docks, the first dock designed for steamships. Owing to fear of fire, it was built some distance north of Prince's Dock. In 1836, the gap was filled by Trafalgar and Victoria Docks. When Clarence closed in 1928 to make way for a power station, its half-tide dock and part of Trafalgar Dock formed a new Trafalgar configuration with a branch dock at the south end. In the early 1970s, Victoria and Trafalgar Branch Dock were filled in to create a new 17-acre terminal for the B&I passenger, car ferry and freight services to Dublin. The Spanish-built B&I container ship *Sligo* (launched 1971, 787 grt) at the terminal under the Freightway crane, on 18 June 1974. In the foreground, the Weaver Storage Company's *Parfield* (1951, 54 nrt) is towing Manchester-registered barges *Colmere* (1948, 54 nrt) and *Linmere* (1951, 56 nrt). When the terminal closed, most of the basin became a landfill site. The narrow passage into Clarence Graving Docks survives, but has been closed since 2005.
Nigel Bowker

RIGHT: Reflecting the port's rapid growth, Hartley's famous five – the interconnected steamship docks Salisbury, Collingwood, Stanley, Nelson and Bramley-Moore – all opened in 1848, with a combined water space of 33 acres and two miles of quays. Salisbury was unique in having passages on three sides, as well as a double river entrance flanking a central island on which stood Victoria Clock Tower, designed by Hartley and Philip Hardwick. Today, the six-face clock in the hexagonal, castellated bell tower no longer works. The provision of a double entrance enabled ships to arrive and depart simultaneously for several hours on either side of a full tide. Also visible are the pier master's and dock master's houses and the cyclopean granite seawalls. *Commercial postcard, courtesy of J. B. Horne*

AERIAL VIEW OF A DOCK ENTRANCE, LIVERPOOL. (631)

THIS PAGE: Named after a chairman of the dock committee, Bramley-Moore was one of the quintet of 1848 docks, while Wellington and its half-tide dock (opened 1849) were named after the victor of Waterloo. Following the opening of the Lancashire & Yorkshire (L&Y) High Level Coal Railway (1856-1966), coal drops were built above the eastern sides of both docks. Later, further sidings and drops occupied the north side of Bramley-Moore. Hydraulic power enabled 4,000 tons of coal a day to be sent for export, for bunkering and to power local industry. In 1895, steam locomotives replaced horses on the high level sidings. To feed Clarence Dock Power Station, coal from pits in Scotland and South Wales was offloaded at Bramley-Moore. Following modernisation at the beginning of the 20th century, Wellington developed as a base for trade with Northern Europe. Following demolition of the High Level Railway, the site became a gravel store, while Bramley-Moore was the base for the Svitzer fleet of tugs and a discharge point for sea-dredged sand and gravel. It also marks the limit of the present dock system. These sequential views taken on the High Level Railway in May 1962 follow the path of a loaded wagon as it progresses by hydraulically-powered turntable, wire and capstan onto the wagon tippler perched above the ship's hold.
J. G. Parkinson,
Online Transport Archive

ABOVE: The only dock on the east side of the dock road now forms part of the Stanley Dock Conservation Area. Among the listed buildings are Hartley's North Warehouse (centre) and his hydraulic power station complete with its tall brick chimney (built 1854). The flight of locks linking it to the Leeds & Liverpool Canal has been used since 2009 by narrow boats making their dockland journey to Albert Dock. The MD&HB Salvage steamer *Vigilant* (launched 1953, 728 grt) is laid up at the north quay on 2 July 1973, together with the buoys *C8*, *Burbo* and *Q14*. *Nigel Bowker*

ABOVE: Named after a local MP, Sandon Dock (opened 1851, ten acres) originally had six graving docks (later consumed by Huskisson Dock, left) on its north side, while Sandon Basin had absorbed the short-lived Wellington Half-Tide Basin. In 1892, a half-tide dock was built together with a wider river entrance, later revised to accommodate the triple entrance and locks seen here. To the right was the High Level Coal Railway. In Huskisson Branch Dock No 1 are the two-storey Cunard Line transit sheds. *Commercial postcard, courtesy of John Horne*

BELOW: On 12 September 1959, accompanied by the Alexandra Towing Company steam tug *Alfred* (launched 1937, 215 grt), the *Port Sydney* (1955, 10,166 grt), a Port Line refrigerated cargo vessel, in Sandon Half-Tide Dock, making for Huskisson with Sandon and Wellington in the background. Although much altered, this vessel still sails under the Panamanian flag as the cruise ship *Ocean Odyssey*. In the background is the funnel of the *Sylvania* (1957, 22,107 grt), one of the Cunard 'quads' associated with Liverpool during the dying years of the liners. Sandon had the MD&HB's first reinforced concrete transit sheds. *H. B. Christiansen, Online Transport Archive*

TOP: During World War 2, the Dock Estate system suffered heavy damage. One of the worst incidents occurred in Huskisson Dock on 2 May 1941, when a deflated barrage balloon set fire to the Brocklebank Line's *Malakand*, berthed in Branch Dock No 2. Loaded with shells and explosives, the ship eventually exploded, its component parts found as far as two and a half miles away. Dating from 1852 and named after William Huskisson MP, the dock had switched from handling bulk timber in 1860 to become the premier Cunard base, until they moved to Gladstone in 1927. During World War 1, three branch docks were added while the main dock and passage into Canada Dock were widened. Post-1927, Huskisson was used for trade with Europe and the importation of sugar and molasses. After the *Malakand* explosion, Branch Dock no 2 was filled in but the other two branches were rebuilt. *Photographer unknown*

MIDDLE: Designed to replace Huskisson as the centre for the importation of North American timber, Canada Dock (opened 1859), Hartley's last dock, had huge yards enabling massive loads to be offloaded from ships moored bow to quay. In 1893, four of these yards went up in flames. The hydraulic machinery to power the 100-foot wide gates and bridges in Canada Lock was housed in a neo-medieval, castle-like tower (foreground), now demolished. The opening in 1862 of Canada Basin (left), with its north and south jetties, only partially alleviated problems with silting and the angle of the entrance. Visible in the background are Canada Branch Dock No 3 (1903), Brocklebank Graving Dock and North Carriers Dock. *Commercial postcard, courtesy of J. B. Horne.*

RIGHT: Seen passing through Canada Lock in 1903 is the twin-screw 'Cunarder' *Lucania* (launched 1893, 12,952 grt). She made her first transatlantic crossing from Liverpool and then, following a fire in Huskisson in 1909, was sent for scrap. Another famous liner to lock out here was the ill-fated 'Cunarder' *Lusitania*, which was fitted with guns in Canada Dock shortly before she was torpedoed in 1915. *H. B. Christiansen collection, Online Transport Archive.*

TOP: Eventually, Canada had three branch docks, the last opening in 1903, as well as a graving dock, giving a total water area of 39 acres. Even though the dock entrance was rebuilt in the 1920s, it was not used until the outbreak of World War 2. Canada was also equipped to supply ships with bunkering and cargo coal. In the 1950s, it was rearranged to accommodate cargo liners; then, as part of a £20 million modernisation programme, the upgraded Langton River Entrance on the north side of Canada Basin was finally opened in 1962. The Alexander Shipping Company's *Shaftesbury* (launched 1958, 8,365 grt) is seen in Branch Dock No 3 on 22 July 1966; timber can also be seen on the quay. Today, the dock's roll on/roll-off berths are no longer used, but it does handle edible oil, general cargoes and scrap metal. *H. B. Christiansen, Online Transport Archive.*

MIDDLE: Most of the large deep-water steamship docks were built in the borough of Bootle. When the latter failed to prevent the MD&HB obtaining a compulsory purchase of its foreshore, the once peaceful village was transformed into 'Brutal Bootle', large sections of which would later be obliterated during World War 2. The first Bootle dock was Canada Half-Tide Dock (opened 1862), which was renamed Brocklebank in 1879 after a former MD&HB chairman. Built for the timber trade, it later absorbed two half-tide branch docks and the two former Canada Carriers Docks, the southern one eventually becoming a graving dock. Substantially rebuilt between 1904-08, it was altered again in the 1950s to benefit from the new Langton River Entrance and is now the terminal for the ferry service to Belfast. Today the site is partially occupied by industrial buildings. In 1968, the *Apapa* was photographed in the branch dock; in the background are the Harland and Wolff workshops on Regent Road. *Nigel Bowker*

LEFT: Designed by G. F. Lyster to be accessible at all stages of the tide for larger draught liners, Langton, Alexandra and Hornby Docks cost £4 million and came complete with concrete-cement walls, modern warehouses, transit sheds, hydraulic cranes, Gothic-style buildings and electric light for night work. Langton (opened 1879) had a branch dock, two graving docks and passages into Brocklebank and Alexandra (later doubled). The original Langton River Entrance, which had two wide locks connecting with Canada Basin, was replaced after years of delay by a new entrance in 1962. The branch and graving docks were subsequently in-filled to provide parking for the Brocklebank ferry terminal. One of the mass-produced American C2 steam turbine merchant ships, the *Sue Lykes* (launched 1945, 8,179 grt) of Lykes Bros, New Orleans, is seen berthed on the north side of the main dock on 2 July 1966. Ahead in the branch dock are three Ellerman & Papayanni Line vessels, the nearest being the *Palmellian* (1948, 1,531 grt). *A. S. Clayton, Online Transport Archive*

ABOVE: Accessed first from Langton and later from Hornby and Gladstone Docks, Alexandra (opened 1881) had a main north-south dock flanked by three substantial east-west branch docks (Nos 1-3). On 5 November 1960, the former White Star liner Britannic (launched 1930, 27,666 grt) is seen being prepared in Branch No 3 for her final round-trip to New York. The first British motor-ship on Atlantic service, she became part of the Cunard/White Star fleet in 1934 but retained her White Star colours until withdrawn. From 1939 to 1947 she was requisitioned as a troopship. Her fore-funnel was a dummy, encasing the wireless room. Alexandra had grain and cold-storage facilities, with the mechanical handling eventually controlled by computer. In the background is a travelling grain elevator. *H. B. Christiansen, Online Transport Archive.*

RIGHT: The east-west Hornby Dock (opened 1883) was accessed initially from Alexandra and named after an MD&HB chairman. Although it lost its north-side timber facilities during construction of Gladstone Graving Dock, it still imported half a million tons a year into the 1960s. Seen in the later passage between Hornby and Gladstone Docks on 1 July 1966 and flying the Liberian flag is the *Pegasus* (launched 1950, 1,932 grt). The motor tug *John Lamey* (1927, 185 grt) was the first diesel ship-handling tug on the Mersey. It had been converted from the older steam tug *Lady Elizabeth* and fitted with a 1943 eight-cylinder Crossley engine. *A. S. Clayton, Online Transport Archive.*

LEFT: Named after Prime Minister Gladstone, the last steamship complex was completed in 1927. Home to scores of memorable liners and altered during World War 2 to accommodate warships, the 56-acre site comprised a gated river entrance with locks, a vestibule dock, Docks 1 and 2 flanked by transit sheds, the largest graving dock in Europe (opened 1913), three miles of quays and a passage into Hornby. Until the early 1960s, multi-gauge tracks laid on the quayside housed locomotives for export. On 28 December 1959, we see Canadian Pacific's *Empress of Britain* (launched 1956, 25,516 grt) and Empress of England (1957, 25,500 grt) are in Dock No 1; also visible are Dock No 2, the corner of the graving dock (1,050 feet long with a 120-foot wide entrance, later used as a temporary container terminal), Seaforth bus terminal and elements of the surrounding rail network. Today, everything is within the Freeport. *Medley & Bird, H. B. Christiansen collection, Online Transport Archive.*

LEFT: On 25 January 1953, the *Empress of Canada*, formerly the *Duchess of Richmond* (launched 1928, 20,000 grt) caught fire in Gladstone. All efforts to save her failed. Made top heavy by water from fire hoses, she slid onto her side. Following Europe's biggest post-war salvage operation, the stricken 'White Empress' was raised and sent for scrap in 1954. *Glynn Parry collection*

RIGHT: Families gather at Gladstone Lock to wave *au revoir* to the crew of the Blue Funnel Line steamship *Perseus* (launched 1950, 10,109 grt), seen here outward bound to the Far East on 1 July 1966. *A. S. Clayton, Online Transport Archive.*

BELOW: Spacious and well equipped for handling bulk cargoes and containers, the Royal Seaforth container terminal opened in 1973 at a cost of £50 million. Subsequently enlarged and upgraded, it now forms part of the highly successful Freeport where imports are handled free of EU taxes, UK customs duty and VAT. Container movements are computer-controlled from within the Maritime Centre at Seaforth. With efficient transport links, the Freeport is part of the Atlantic Gateway regeneration scheme aimed at revitalising the surrounding area. Today, the dock handles half a million containers a year, a quarter of the container traffic between the UK and USA, some 2½ million tons of grain and animal feed, over 1¼ million tons of edible oils and just over 450,000 tons of timber. Here, the *Panary* (launched 1937, 167 grt) and the *Dowlais D* (1985, 794 grt) are loading Canadian wheat in the grain arm of the dock on 3 January 2008. *Nigel Bowker*

MERSEY DOCKS & HARBOUR BOARD VESSELS

To keep the docks, port and approaches fully operational, the MD&HB maintained a varied fleet of floating units ranging from dredgers, floating cranes and pilot boats to barges, flats and launches. Glimpses of the fleet appear elsewhere, but these few views illustrate something of their range and variety.

RIGHT: Self-propelled floating cranes with various lifting capacities played a vital role at the docks. The former Ministry of War floating crane *Birket* (launched 1942, acquired 1946) is seen in Brunswick Dock in the 1960s. Capable of lifting 60 tons, it is lowering Ghana Railways diesel locomotive No 1852 onto an Elder Dempster's 'K' class vessel. Once on deck, riggers would see it securely stowed. *GEC Alsthom Archive*

BELOW: The dredger *Leviathan* (1909-62, 8,590 grt) was once the largest in the world. *John Collingwood collection*

LEFT: An organised independent pilot service for the Mersey existed from 1766. Eventually, pilot boats were stationed from Anglesey to the Liverpool Bar. A Liverpool pilot boat spent a week at a bar station, a week ferrying mail and pilots to other pilot boats, a week in dock for repair and inspection and another week to refuel and take on provisions. Seen moored in Collingwood Dock in 1968 is the diesel-electric Liverpool Pilot No 3, the *Arnet Robinson* (launched 1958, 734 grt). Sold in 1982, she was broken up in India in 2004. *J. G. Parkinson, Online Transport Archive*

ABOVE: Seen here in 1967, salvage vessels like the *Salvor* (launched 1947, 671 grt) monitored the docks and river and undertook routine observation and maintenance of buoys and lightships in Liverpool Bay. Withdrawn as the last working steamer on the river, her mast and derricks now stand opposite St Nicholas Church. *Marcus Eavis, Online Transport Archive*

RIGHT: The most powerful floating crane was *Mammoth* (launched 1920, 1,542 grt), with its huge jib capable of lifting 200 tons. After it was sunk during World War 2, Winston Churchill apparently insisted it was raised and repaired. Here it is seen removing the landing stage on 25 July 1973. After leaving the Mersey in 1986, this veteran remains hard at work as the *Baltic Mammoth* in Scandinavian waters. *Glynn Parry*

DOCK WORKFORCE

Until 1949, most Liverpool dockers were casual workers with no guarantee of employment. For decades, the culture of 'casualism' and docker gangs prevailed. Hundreds congregated twice a day at MD&HB control points or 'pens', hoping for work. The pens on the Liverpool side were numbered 1-11, with those offering the most work being 5 and 6 (Canada and Huskisson Docks) and 10 (King's and Queen's Docks). Some were controlled by powerful, often biased, foremen who could give preferential treatment to family and friends, as well as those of the same religious persuasion or ethnic background. A common method of supplementing wages was by pilferage.

To obtain work before World War 2, most men needed a 'button' (the union badge) and a 'tally' (the right to work). When given work, each man received a second tally which the timekeeper used to log the hours worked, payment usually being made later from four major clearing houses located in streets close to the dock road. Before World War 1, some payments had been made in pubs. Night work sometimes meant longer hours and better money.

The well-paid waterfront aristocracy included master stevedores and master porters. In the 19th and early 20th centuries, labour in the independent south docks was mostly contracted out to small firms who hired labour as required, whereas in the north end the master stevedores and porters tended to be nominees of the major steamship companies. In the broadest terms, stevedores worked the ships and porters the quayside. With the advance of mechanisation (it took some 10,600 working hours to load and unload a conventional cargo liner, as opposed to 550 working hours for an 11,000-ton container ship), thousands of skilled and unskilled dock-related jobs disappeared.

Historically, labour relations on the docks were poor. During part of the 1911 transport strike, the port had effectively been controlled by a union strike committee. Post-war, matters were hardly helped by waves of unofficial strikes. During the 1960s and 1970s, increasingly militant stoppages occurred as the labour force fought to prevent mass unemployment, with some strikes aimed at union officials as well as employers. As a result shipping lines simply deserted Liverpool, leading to the eventual economic collapse of the MD&HB. The abolition of the National Dock Labour Scheme in 1989 and a lengthy lock-out in the late 1990s ended organised labour in the docks. Today, many of the 800 or so people working in the docks are once again employed on a casual basis.

Overseeing transfers from ship to quayside were the stevedores who fell into three groups. Issuing instructions were 'the men at the rail': 'winchmen' operated winches and derricks while 'holdsmen' were on deck or in the hold; the work in the hold itself was undertaken by 'lumpers'.

Over the years, British firms exported a wide range of road and rail vehicles through Liverpool. This English Electric-bodied AEC664T 3-axle trolleybus is seen in Alexandra Dock in 1937, being stowed onboard the SS *Luga* bound ultimately for Moscow, where the design was copied and several replica vehicles produced. *Stuart Marsh*

ABOVE: Commodities leaving the quayside were monitored and recorded by the porters. First, the quay porters handled the goods; 'checkers' then checked everything, 'weighers' logged weight on MD&HB scales and 'markers' recorded details of each item with a marking brush. In this bustling 1933 scene, all manner of sacks, barrels, boxes, cartons and pallets are on the move. Roof-mounted hoists served the upper levels of many MD&HB warehouses. *Photographer unknown*

ABOVE: Many long-established waterfront industries such as milling, cooperage, pottery, whale oil refining, shipbuilding and foundries disappeared with expansion of the docks. One of the last to survive was the fishing fleet. Fishermen are repairing nets in Canning Dock here, just months before the last trawlers left the river in 1939. *J. E. Marsh*

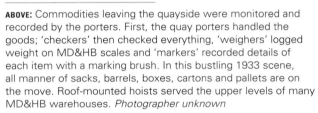

RIGHT: Jobs which posed serious health risks included removing chaff and dust from ships' holds, using long brushes dripping with red lead to paint ship's hulls in exposed graving docks ('pneumonia coffins') where the slippery surfaces were often treacherous. Coast Lines' *Pacific Coast* (launched 1947, 1,188 grt) is seen here in one of the Langton graving docks in July 1966. (None of the men wears any form of protective clothing.) Capable of holding vessels up to 950 feet long, this graving dock could be divided into smaller areas as seen here. *A. S. Clayton, Online Transport Archive.*

HYDRAULIC POWER, POLICE, CUSTOMS & EXCISE

ABOVE: First introduced at Albert Dock in 1848, hydraulic power revolutionised the movement of machinery from cranes and wagon turntables to dock gates and bridges. Clean, safe and noise-free, some of these former hydraulic power stations still remain. To supply the city, the Liverpool Hydraulic Power Company had two pump houses (Boundary Street and Grafton Street) circulating water round a network of pipes to serve cranes, hoists and lifts. This view shows the smaller of the two pumping stations just to the right of the large, column-guided gasholder on Grafton Street (1847). The vacant industrial sites, cleared except for their tall chimneys, once belonged to Mersey Forge. Also visible are (right) Dyson trailers, pioneers of intermodal road/rail vehicles, the corporation refuse destructor with its very tall chimney (right centre) and a windmill (top centre) with its steam-driven successors in High Park Mills. *Photographer unknown*

LEFT: Until merger with the Liverpool police force in 1837, the docks had their own police. From 1852 to 1976, they were variously policed by the fire brigade, the River Mersey police and the city police force. Since 1976, jurisdiction has been vested in the Port of Liverpool police.

This former customs depot at Toxteth, one of several serving the Dock Estate, housed both branches of the Customs & Excise service – the 'Waterguard' and land and shipping officers, who until 1971 were answerable to the collector in the main Custom House (for Custom & Excise purposes, the UK was divided into 'collections'). Wearing Royal Navy-derived uniforms, the former boarded vessels to apprehend smugglers, search for contraband and prohibited goods, and to deal with the crew and passengers, while the latter wore no uniform but were assisted by 'watchers' who did, but without the customary gold braid. They examined and cleared exported/imported goods on the quayside and in warehouses. *Jonathan Cadwallader*

THE DOCK ROAD

Consisting of a number of named thoroughfares, the main artery running the length of the Dock Estate was known locally as 'the Dock Road'. In its heyday, the east side was dominated by railway goods stations, refineries, cold storage units, coal and timber yards, ship repairers, warehouses, factories, stables and saw mills, gas works, engine and boiler works, export packers, pubs, hotels and brothels. Within striking distance were premises for receiving, storing and processing grain, timber, coal, leather and sugar. In close proximity to (or intermixed with) all this smoke and grime were massed areas of low-quality housing. On the west side was the Dock Estate with its many entrances, warehouses, silos and cold storage units. Adjacent to it was The Line of Docks Railway and, immediately above, the unique Liverpool Overhead Railway. In the central waterfront area, the Dock Road was overlooked by stylish office blocks, warehouses and the backs of the major Pier Head buildings.

For several years after World War 2, queues of lorries mingled with horse-drawn carts, steam lorries and slow-moving trains. However, as the docks declined so did traffic levels, with sections of the road falling into disrepair. Today, some stretches are no longer recognisable.

TOP: Supervised by the dock police, sometimes round the clock, each gate had signs detailing the docks and quays served. Seen here on 31 July 1967, a British Road Services (BRS) Leyland Octopus turns into the entrance for quays 83-98 located at Alexandra, Hornby and Gladstone Docks, its cargo carefully roped under tarpaulins. Seen leaving is a Morris FG K60. *Peter J. Davies*

BOTTOM: As there was no signalling on The Line of Docks Railway, a policeman or flagman (with red and green flags) controlled trains crossing the Dock Road. Here, MD&HB No 11 edges a transfer freight train out of Canada Dock's goods station in 1965. A bell which rang continuously was worked from the connecting rod on the locomotive by a rocker arm. Built by Hunslet in 1940, this inside-cylinder 0-6-0 saddle tank was one of the last dock board engines in regular use. *B. D. Pyne, Online Transport Archive.*

TOP: Steam waggons were seen regularly on the dock road. Passing the old order in 1955 is a Sentinel DG4 steam tractor (built in 1930), owned by John Taylor & Sons of Union Street. The carter may well have nipped into *The King Hal*, the Bent's public house seen in the background. Negotiating the turn from Regent Road is a Tate & Lyle truck making for the firm's refinery on Love Lane. Behind the hoardings (right) is the old LMS Sandon and Canada goods station. *Marcus Eavis, Online Transport Archive.*

MIDDLE: Passing the White Star Building at the foot of James Street, this steam waggon is crossing the busy junction with Mann Island on 3 November 1951. This is No 11 in the fleet of haulage contractor William Harper & Sons. Suited to short runs with few gradients, the vertical boiler is in the cab and the steam engine under the load platform. Until 1957, the Sentinel Steam Waggon Company had a repair facility in Duke's Dock. The last steam waggon was withdrawn in 1962. *J. H. Meredith*

BOTTOM: One of the oldest stretches of the Dock Road is Wapping. This was the site of the first rail link into the docks laid between Wapping (later Park Lane) goods station and King's Dock. The original section of the Line of Docks Railway (built 1849) is seen heading northwards. By the time of the photograph, 8 June 1969, Park Lane was no longer served by rail. On its outer wall is a long-defunct drinking fountain, while a knot of women and children wait for a bus towards the Dingle. *Cedric Greenwood*

THE LINE OF DOCKS RAILWAY

The railway revolution spread like wildfire in Liverpool. The first section of the horse-operated Line of Docks Railway opened in 1849, to speed the movement of goods in and out of the docks and between the mainline goods stations. However, it took five animals to move six wagons, although this was later increased to 12 wagons when larger teams were harnessed. Until the opening of the Liverpool Overhead Railway (LOR) in 1893, for a period the line also carried two million passengers a year in 'omnibuses on wheels', which were able to leave the rails and pass goods trains.

Operations were transformed in 1895, when the MD&HB permitted company-owned locos to operate regularly over its line. Detailed regulations covered speed, distance between trains, number of wagons and the equipment to be fitted to each locomotive, which included a spark arrestor, baffle plate (to divert smoke away from the underneath of the LOR) and a warning bell. A man also had to walk in front of each train throughout its entire journey.

When the MD&HB started operating its own locomotives in 1905, mainline engines only ventured onto the line when working between company goods stations. Agreements now covered haulage charges, the arranging and allocating of berths, goods carried, the number of wagons and assembly of trainloads, as well as the movement of mainline wagons in and out and around the Dock Estate. A chain of command linked the Dock Board's chief traffic manager with a range of inspectors responsible for different areas within the estate.

An extension was built to serve Gladstone Dock in 1927 and new sidings were laid into Clarence Dock Power Station in 1931. During World War 2 the 80-mile system was at full capacity, with most bomb damage being swiftly repaired. As docks closed and new technology took over, rail traffic declined, with tonnage dwindling from four million in 1944 to just 150,000 by 1972. Although all MD&HB rail operation ended in 1973, the section of line north from Alexandra Dock now carries traffic to and from the Freeport.

In this delightful picture, MD&HB No 1 – an Avonside outside cylinder 0-6-0 saddle tank of 1904 – has received permission to take its assorted wagons to various assigned shipping berths. It has left the former L&Y North Mersey goods station and is on the Line of Docks Railway with another Dock Board engine approaching from the south. This historic locomotive is one of the exhibits in the new Museum of Liverpool. *B. D. Pyne, Online Transport Archive.*

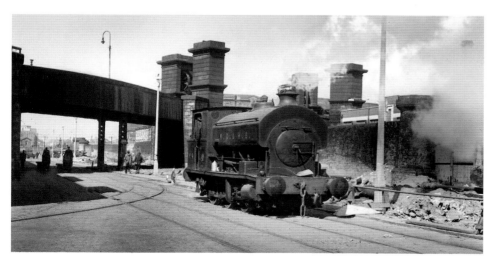

TOP: On 29 April 1964, No 11 (Hunslet, inside-cylinder 0-6-0ST, built 1940) departs Bankfield goods station and is about to cross Regent Road under the watchful eye of the man with the obligatory red flag. This yard had extensive cold storage for imported meat. The MD&HB had several locomotive sheds along the dock estate. *B. Faragher*

MIDDLE: Separate road and rail bridges spanned the passage between Collingwood and Stanley Docks. The original rail bridge, widened in 1877 to accommodate double track, was replaced in 1893 by a superb example of Victorian ingenuity. This was a two-level combined lift and swing bridge; the leaves of the lower deck could be raised sufficiently to allow small vessels to pass through, without disrupting the LOR on the upper deck. If a larger vessel needed to use the passage, then the whole structure was raised. By 1962, the upper level had been removed. The rake of 'empties' seen here is coming from Clarence Dock power station. When this lower deck was removed in 1970, the railway was cut in two. *J. G. Parkinson, Online Transport Archive.*

BOTTOM: Shortly before withdrawal in 1964, No 4 (Avonside, outside cylinder 0-6-0ST, built 1930) is shown on the south side of the lifting bridge, carrying the High Level Coal Railway over Regent Road. A much cruder structure than the one at Stanley Dock, the rusting wheels for the balance chains can still be seen, although the bridge had been locked in position since 1940. Aimed at minimising the risk of fire, these locomotives had meshed spark arrestors. They always carried two short shovels blade down, one on the front fender and one on the cab roof. Feeding the fire in these narrow cabs required skill – even with a stunted shovel. *B. D. Pyne, Online Transport Archive.*

TOP: The High Level Coal Railway provided an excellent vantage point from which to photograph No 9 (Hunslet inside cylinder 0-6-0ST, 1940) on 10 May 1962, its bell tolling continuously as it heads a northbound train of clanking empties from Clarence Dock power station. To help these sturdy workhorses to take the strain from a standing start, the 20-ton steel hoppers had extra-long couplings.
J. G. Parkinson,
Online Transport Archive.

RIGHT: A city worker in her elegant two-piece suit ignores No 34 (Hunslet, 0-6-0, built 1951) as it approaches the busy Water Street crossing in 1956. The Liverpool Arms at the north end of the Goree Warehouses is still open and the poster attached to the Overhead Railway stanchion advertises a local rugby union match, between Birkenhead Park and New Brighton.
J. G. Todd,
Online Transport Archive.

LIVERPOOL OVERHEAD RAILWAY (LOR) 1893-1956

Although little remains today of the LOR which once ran 16 feet above the Dock Road, this unique line is still remembered with genuine affection and has been the subject of several books and a best-selling DVD. During the 1850s, various proposals to improve passenger movements along the Dock Road included a railway running on the roofs of transit sheds. Influenced by the steam-operated elevated railways in New York, the LOR went one better in becoming the first of its kind to be electrically powered.

To tap additional residential traffic, by 1905 the seven-mile line linked Dingle with Seaforth and Litherland, where connections were made with the recently electrified L&Y Liverpool-Southport service. The LOR stations at Pier Head, James Street and Custom House were close to the city's business and commercial districts. As the viaduct was directly over the Line of Docks Railway, the area beneath was nicknamed 'the dockers' umbrella'.

Although there were differences, with some carriages later modified and others modernised, 46 motors cars were delivered between 1891-95 and a variety of trailers between 1895-1936. Alterations to the live rails enabled L&Y lightweight units to operate a short-lived service over the LOR to Dingle. In the early 1920s, colour-light signalling replaced automatic semaphores, although signal boxes were still needed at Dingle and in the vicinity of the two sheds. To attract additional revenue, striking posters highlighting the line's unrivalled views of the docks and the ships were produced, as well as a comprehensive range of tickets.

While trade flourished the line prospered, but during economic downturns passenger numbers slumped as unemployment escalated. For example, in 1917, 17 million were carried, but by 1933 the numbers had decreased to 5½ million. However, during World War 2 there was a steep climb back to 14 million. The structure was frequently damaged and both James Street and Prince's Dock stations were destroyed, with the latter remaining closed. Interestingly, both the military and the LMS Railway wanted the line demolished. Liverpool Corporation also stated they could provide sufficient buses but would need additional fuel. Unknown to the LOR management, they were also deliberately kept waiting for replacement steel.

Due to an oversight, the line was not nationalised in 1948. Unable to afford new rolling stock, the company built replacement bodies for eight three-car sets between 1947 and 1955. After the war, passenger numbers again tumbled, although the LOR was still carrying 25,000 a day in the mid-1950s. Faced by the high cost of renewing the decaying structure and unable to secure any financial assistance, the company opted for closure, the last trains running on 30 December 1956.

Together with two preserved coaches (one of which will be exhibited in the Museum of Liverpool) and some truncated stanchions, the most significant remains from the LOR are Dingle station and tunnel (1896), the site now occupied by a car repair firm. Carved through sandstone and ending against a vertical wall of rock, the half-mile tunnel is 52 feet at its greatest width and 24 feet 6 inches high. Controlled by a signal box, the station had an island platform and several sidings. This historic last-night view was taken on 30 December 1956.
R. S. Stephens, Online Transport Archive.

ABOVE: After 1914, the standard formation was a motorcar at either end of a shorter trailer. Approaching Herculaneum station in May 1955 is one of 30 motor cars built in 1891, of which ten, including No 27, were widened in 1902/3 with the addition of a full driver's compartment, giving a total of 198 seats including 48 in first class used mainly by city workers and tourists. Most of the dockscape has disappeared, although the railway tracks (far right) are now part of the electrified Northern Line service.
Ray DeGroote,
Online Transport Archive

MIDDLE: This is one of the sets given replacement bodies with upgraded seating and air-operated doors between 1947-55. This area suffered considerable wartime damage, although Wapping Warehouse (left) and the Baltic Fleet pub (right) remain today.
Ray DeGroote,
Online Transport Archive

BOTTOM: Resting at Seaforth Sands station (built 1905) in 1955 is No 4-47-17, with its total of 204 seats. Close by are the workshop and main depot (1926) which incorporated part of the original station (1894). From 1900-25, this was the starting point of an LOR feeder tram service to Waterloo and Great Crosby. Today, nothing remains of this once busy transport hub. *W. G. S. Hyde,*
Online Transport Archive

LEFT: Older Liverpudlians will recall how the LOR snaked behind the three Pier Head buildings. In 1948, a photographer standing in the Liver Building took this remarkable shot of three forms of transport – a tram, a Dock Board locomotive under the 'dockers' umbrella' and an LOR train accelerating from Pier Head station (left). Most stations were fairly basic, with steep steps up from the road, but Pier Head (the busiest on the line) and Custom House had canopies over their platforms while a few others had footbridges.
W. M. Price, courtesy of Geoff Price

BELOW: Each Grand National day, the LOR trains ran to Aintree, Sefton Arms, over tracks originally electrified by the L&Y. Sparking their way along the rusty third rail, these LOR specials terminated at platform three. After delivering its morning load of punters in March 1956, as seen here, No 19-16-7 will return at the end of the day for a trip to Dingle.
R. S. Stephens,
Online Transport Archive

CARTERS

For decades, the carters were one of the most powerful labour groups in Liverpool. Much has been written about the city's sectarian divide; but before World War 1, the vast majority of the 11,000 carters would have been non-Catholics, employed mostly by Protestant-owned companies who set cartage rates for moving all manner of goods.

A skilled carter could control his horses purely by words and signals. Some beasts proved so reliable that they carried on plodding forward, allowing their carter to nod off or nip into a pub for a swift half (or more). Although horsepower was cost-effective, moving anything up to 15 tons over short distances, haulage contractors gradually switched to lorries, vans and steam waggons after World War 1, but a few firms had stables, horses and carters into the early 1970s.

BELOW: Seen here on 16 July 1913, descendants of powerful Flemish draught horses plod along the Dock Road, their carters wearing the traditional long leather apron and cloth cap. At this time, over 40,000 horses were owned by Liverpool carters.

The *Liverpool Arms* at the north end of the Goree Warehouses once served whisky in earthenware teapots. Known latterly as *Tom Hall's*, it closed in 1958. Giving way for yet another new bank, the building on the corner of Water Street and Back Goree had replaced an early Custom House, while Tower Buildings (left) was named in memory of a fourteenth-century tower demolished in 1819, when Water Street was widened. En route to the Pier Head was a posh first-class tram. Resplendent in their cream and gold livery, these ran selected routes from 1908 to 1923, with passengers paying a premium fare to travel in the plush lower saloon. *Liverpool City Engineers*

LEFT: As late as 1969, cart no 27 in the fleet of brewers, Magee Marshall, was still active. *J. G. Parkinson, Online Transport Archive.*

RAILWAY COMPANIES AND THE DOCKS

In this age of containerisation and bulk movements, it is difficult to imagine the thousands of men once engaged in the complex, time-consuming procedures which covered the transhipment of goods to and from the miles of quays within the Dock Estate. '*Forwarding Merchandise Traffic*', a pamphlet issued by the L&NWR in the 1920s, offers some fascinating detail on this.

A district goods manager based at Waterloo goods station on Great Howard Street had overall control and was also responsible for the bill of lading and enquiry offices in the city centre. The focal point of operations was the massive marshalling point at Edge Hill, from where goods were transferred to and from the Company's goods stations on the Dock Road. Each dock and each Liverpool district had its own assigned goods station, each with warehouse accommodation and listed crane power (Canada Dock had the most powerful, at 40 tons) while Canada and Waterloo also had major cattle facilities. Although most of the traffic to and from Liverpool was by rail, fleets of company-owned carts and lorries transferred goods to and from ships and warehouses either at the goods stations or around the city. However, owing to the entrenched power of the independent carters, very few mainline wagons were loaded or unloaded at the quayside.

Any load over one ton was despatched directly from Edge Hill to the named goods station. However, smaller loads could, in certain circumstances, be sent to one goods station to be forwarded to another, although consignments could not be split between two stations. Transfers along the Line of Docks Railway between Park Lane and Waterloo goods stations were undertaken by the L&NWR (later LMS and BR) locos. Anything over two tons heading for a dock with a rail berth connection had to be loaded separately at Edge Hill and marked 'haulage traffic'. Movements such as the return of empty meat wrappers to Canada Dock and empty grain sacks to Waterloo had their own specific rules.

A 'list of favour' gave priority and preferential rates to scores of Liverpool-based firms, including major steamship lines. These companies were allocated a pre-assigned goods station from which their merchandise was transferred by rail or road. Shipments could not be sent to Edge Hill and could only be accepted when consigned to a specific goods station, dock or ship. For those not on the list, their merchandise, such as perishables requiring prompt delivery, could be despatched to Edge Hill.

GOODS STATIONS

Following the Liverpool & Manchester Railway's investment in the world's first freight-only tunnel (built 1830), other companies anxious to tap the lucrative dock traffic built a range of goods stations, reached mostly by steeply-graded, heavily-engineered branch lines.

Most traffic to and from the docks was either assembled or broken down in massive, company-owned marshalling yards. From these yards, endless short-haul trainloads of hoppers, wagons and vans worked to and from the goods stations. Until agreement with the MD&HB in 1905, company locos entered the Dock Estate via the Line of Docks Railway. Sidings also served many foundries, factories, granaries and mills. During World War 2, all the rail lines worked to maximum capacity, often around the clock, with some sections sustaining severe structural damage from enemy action.

The inevitable switch to road transport, the closure of outdated docks and the introduction of containerisation led to closure of the goods stations. Today, only the container base at Garston remains busy, while the upgraded former L&NWR Bootle branch through Alexandra Dock goods station handles bulk and container traffic from the north docks.

These next views show some of the goods stations, starting at the south end.

ABOVE: In 1968, a BR 9F 2-10-0 snakes out of Brunswick Goods Yard (Cheshire Lines Committee, 1865-1971) onto the mainline from Liverpool Central, with a rake of oil tankers from the nearby Dingle oil terminal accessed via Herculaneum Dock. Formerly, there had been two locomotive depots at this location, the last one closing in 1961, the wall of which is behind the '9F'. *Martin Jenkins, Online Transport Archive.*

MIDDLE: The impressive 16,000 square feet of CLC Brunswick goods station, demolished in 1972, included covered loading bays, ample storage and high-arched entrances facing Sefton Street. Tucked in the northwest corner was the original three-storey passenger terminus (1864-1874) of the Garston & Liverpool Railway which carried the legend, 'Brunswick Station, Cheshire Lines Railway', while the main building had 'Cheshire Lines' boldly emblazoned on its northern face and 'Great Northern, Manchester Sheffield & Lincolnshire & Midland Railway' on its western face. Close by was the L&Y South Docks goods station, destroyed in the Blitz. *J. M. Ryan*

RIGHT: Linking Edge Hill to Wapping goods station, Wapping Dock Tunnel (constructed 1826-1829) is a major industrial archaeological site. Unfortunately, it is now blocked off and the original winding houses in Wapping Cutting have been demolished. Designed by George Stephenson (1781-1848), the 22-foot wide/17-foot high/1¼-mile tunnel provided promoters of the Liverpool & Manchester Railway with access to the docks. Cut through red sandstone with a ruling gradient of 1:48, it was gas-lit on its opening and had whitewashed walls.

ABOVE: A variety of ventilator shafts were built for the tunnel. This one has been demolished. *Neil Cossons*

MIDDLE LEFT: This 1962 photograph shows the western portal of the tunnel. With the replacement of hemp cables by stronger steel versions, the number of loaded wagons that could be hauled up the tunnel increased from six to 16, until locomotive haulage took over in 1896. However, until the tunnel closed, on the descent wagons still followed gravity downhill but with special six-wheeled brake vans attached. As the goods station was in a cutting, wagons were parked under trapdoors in the upper storage areas. *J. G. Parkinson, Online Transport Archive*

MIDDLE RIGHT: Branch tunnels at the northeast end forked into different sections of the extensive complex, with most internal wagon movements by capstan. The goods station closed to rail in 1965 and to all other traffic in 1972. *J. G. Parkinson, Online Transport Archive*

BOTTOM: For transfers between goods stations, company (later BR) locos used the Line of Docks Railway. On the section behind the main waterfront buildings, speed was 4mph as opposed to the normal 6mph and a flagman controlled all road crossings. To reduce delays, the maximum wagonload was 19, increased to 31 after 10pm. Seen making a transfer in 1954 is an ex-L&Y short-wheelbase 0-4-0ST (1891-1910), ideal for tackling sharp curves. These once-familiar little 'pugs' had hinged baffles over their chimneys to divert smoke from the underside of the LOR. Maximum headroom was 17 feet 1 inch. *J. B. C. McCann, Online Transport Archive*

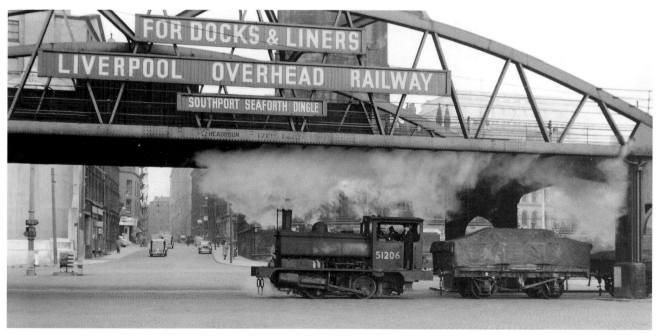

TOP: This magnificent overview of Great Howard Street goods station (1848-1963), the one-time administrative headquarters of L&Y freight operations in Liverpool, shows a sprawling rabbit warren of tracks and sidings (some on two levels) with many tight radius curves – requiring small, specialised locomotives. At the north end, the approach into the goods station (left) and Exchange Station (right) passed over the top of the low-level L&NWR branch feeding into their Waterloo goods station. Movement of wagons into and around the covered goods station (left) was by capstan and turntable. In the bottom left corner is the David Lewis Northern Hospital. *A. S. Clayton, Online Transport Archive*

MIDDLE: Determined to challenge the north-end supremacy of the L&NWR and the L&Y, the CLC built Huskisson goods station (1880-1979). Reached by a two-mile branch with deep cuttings, tunnels and gradients of 1:80, the 25-acre site eventually included offices, sheds, wharves, hydraulic cranes and a basic passenger station (as seen here) from which a short-lived passenger service ran to Liverpool Central (1880-85). Later, the station was absorbed into the yard's extensive cattle-handling facilities. From 1882-1969, a spur connected with Sandon and Canada Dock goods station (built by Midland Railway, 1874) on the Dock Road. *J. M. Ryan*

BOTTOM: The L&NWR had two enormous north end goods stations – Canada Dock (1866-1982) and Alexandra (1881-1967). Heavy freight loads left from both and reached Edge Hill's 'gridiron' via the company's five-mile Bootle branch. Passenger services also connected both to Lime Street. The service from Canada Dock (1870-1941) ended abruptly when bombs breached the Leeds & Liverpool Canal, causing water to flood the goods yard. The passenger station survived until the early 1990s. The Alexandra passenger service lasted until 1948; some ten years later, the derelict station can be seen here complete with name-board, single platform and long overall roof intact. *R. S. Stephens, Online Transport Archive*

LEFT: Sandwiched between the two L&NWR yards was the L&Y's Bankfield and Canada goods station (1871-1965). Seen here on 10 August 1963, Hughes 2-6-0 'Crab' No 42878 waits beside the United Mersey Ships & Stores warehouse, ready to take the steeply-graded mile-long branch (opened 1887) back to Aintree. To the left of the Ford Popular is a rake of refrigerated meat vans and, in Canada Dock, the Elder Dempster freighter *Apapa* (launched 1948, 11607 grt). *J. G. Parkinson, Online Transport Archive*

BELOW: The L&Y North Mersey & Alexandra Dock Goods Station (1866-1968) was another mammoth yard covering the north-end docks and associated industries. It included a four-storey warehouse, sheds, offices, swathes of sidings and a travelling crane capable of lifting heavy baulks of timber. Whilst some long-distance freight did depart directly from the yard, most movements were short-haul trips to and from Aintree sorting sidings along the L&Y's North Mersey Branch (seen in the background). *Martin Jenkins, Online Transport Archive*

WAREHOUSES

Liverpool was a city of warehouses. Of the hundreds of one-time 'storehouses of empire', only a few remain, with just a handful still fulfilling their original function of storing, protecting and distributing a wide range of commodities.

RIGHT: Some 18th-century merchants had warehouse space attached or adjacent to their homes. A secure warehouse away from unprotected quays and sheds prevented pilferage. This rare building on the corner of Seel Street and Colquitt Street was built about 1799 by Thomas Parr, a wealthy merchant and banker.
Jonathan Cadwallader

RIGHT: As trade increased, a rich variety of warehouses, some as tall as 11 storeys, was built. Early examples often had wooden floors and roofs; many were crammed too close together, sometimes amidst overcrowded slums. Fire was a recurring problem, with over 140 conflagrations occurring around the docks in 1842, mostly in warehouses. Following the Liverpool Warehouse Act of 1843, each new warehouse was registered according to the materials used, with insurance companies offering reduced premiums for fireproof buildings. Some of these 19th-century structures resembled the mills and factories of industrial Lancashire. Significant concentrations existed on or close to the east side of the Dock Road, some in rows, some in cramped spaces, many with a date or a company name picked out in brickwork.
Jonathan Cadwallader

LEFT: During World War 2, scores of warehouses were damaged or destroyed. A few were repaired or patched up, but many others were left empty or knocked down, although, in 1946, the Liverpool Warehousing Company still advertised 'Special Warehouses Free and Bonded for Cereals, Cotton, Silk, Hides, Oils, Provisions, Rubber, Sugar, Tea, Wool, Plywood, Canned Goods & General Merchandise'. Slowly, however, modern technology, economic restraints, containerisation, changing trade patterns and the demand for rapid dockside dispersal would end the need for transit warehousing. Survivors from an earlier era include the fireproof Clarence warehouses on Great Howard Street. Designed by P. W. Brancker and opened in the mid-1840s, these typify the safer type of brick and stone construction with firewalls, cast iron windowsills and lintels and sheet iron internal and external doors. Exuding indestructibility and impregnability, they have narrow, recessed breaks for the crane hoists, rounded corners to minimise damage, small windows and a long, steep, narrow stairwell lit by tiny openings.
Jonathan Cadwallader

BELOW: These fireproof warehouses, now demolished, had replaced earlier examples consumed in 1842 by a ferocious fire which started in nearby Formby Street and devastated a grim area of tightly-packed factories, mills and slums, killing several and destroying goods (mostly cotton) and property to the value of £350,000. Photographed on Barton Street in April 1974, they latterly formed part of the extensive J. Bibby's complex, with their canopies extending over the loading bays and interconnecting walkways as later additions. *Cedric Greenwood*

RIGHT: On 1 August 1966, a box is hoisted from a parked Leyland Octopus and trailer, owned by McCready Bros of Liverpool, into one of a row of mid-19th-century warehouses (since demolished) on New Quay. Rising directly from the edge of the road, the warehouses were owned at this time by local shipping and forwarding agents Henry Diaper. Other warehouses and a couple of pubs had been demolished in the late 1920s to make space for the dock branch of the Queensway Tunnel (right). *Peter J. Davies*

BELOW LEFT: An artistic view of the rusticated arcade of the Goree Warehouses (1803). These classical blocks, which followed the architectural lines of 18th-century houses, stood on the east side of the former George's Dock (right). They were associated with the infamous triangular trade and were named after a West African slave port. Having superseded Bristol, a quarter of all Liverpool ships were involved in transporting slaves. During the 15 months before abolition, 185 Liverpool-based ships carried over 44,000 slaves. After abolition, much of the city's wealth would be derived from slave-worked cotton and tobacco plantations in the USA. By the 1930s, the various upper floors above the arcaded piazzas were occupied by everything from tea and dining rooms to the Warrington Wire Rope Works' offices. *Photographer unknown*

BELOW RIGHT: Looking down Fenwick Street after the May blitz of 1941, with the site of the Corn Exchange (left) on which a new exchange would be erected (1953-59), complete with trading floor and reading room. Surviving structures included the White Star building (left) and the Goree Warehouses, though these were badly damaged and finally demolished in 1958. Fenwick Street, which once ended at the water's edge, was formerly the location for the town's first hackney carriages.
Online Transport Archive

FAR LEFT: Not all warehouse space was instantly obvious. For example, a number of office blocks were built with large basements for storage, their goods being raised and lowered by hydraulically-powered cast-iron teagles (cranes) located on the outside walls. During economic downturns these could house commodities such as cotton, waiting for the market to improve. *Pam Eaton*

LEFT: Former warehouses can still be found dotted around the older parts of the city, some having been converted into residences. *Peter Waller*

BELOW: The mainline railways all owned central area warehouses. For example, the Midland Railway Receiving Warehouse (1872-1874), designed by Culshaw and Sumners, was built near the market area and handled different loads of perishables which arrived from various goods stations by horse and cart (later by lorry), passing through its high-arched doors to be sorted and distributed. Today, it is the National Museum's Conservation Centre. Seen in September 1979, a bus is navigating the gyratory system on its way to the bus station, while on the far left is the former General Post Office (built 1899), designed in French chateau style by Henry Tanner. The building was damaged during the war and now only sections remain. *G. Davies, Online Transport Archive*

RIGHT: One significant architectural loss, demolished during the 1960s, was the six-storey Duke's Dock warehouse. Dating from 1811, this large, Georgian, brick-built edifice had cast-iron beams and columns and a rusticated stone base. *John Collingwood collection*

OPPOSITE TOP: The waterfront around Canning Place was once a clutter of warehouses, offices, small factories, shops and residences. When the Custom House was torn down, the site was vacant until construction in the 1960s of Steers House (seen far right). In 2000 this made way for Liverpool One, which incorporates some sections of the recently excavated remains of New Dock. *Nigel Bowker*

BELOW: In March 1974, an early five-storey warehouse with a gable roof over the hoisting gear stood in Mercer Court, one of the long-vanished maze of alleys and narrow streets north of Canning Place. *Nigel Bowker*

OPPOSITE BOTTOM: Restored examples of monumentally styled, late 19th-century multiple-unit warehouses, with towering elevations incorporating ten loading bays. *Jonathan Cadwallader*

WAREHOUSEMEN

Warehouses provided another source of employment for skilled, semiskilled and unskilled men. At one point, some 10,000 were working in cotton warehouses. However, work was erratic. Sometimes, when it was full or awaiting a consignment, a warehouse could lie dormant for days or months. As on the docks, some 'casuals' were hired directly from stands and, although every effort was made to prevent pilferage, some warehousemen were adept at various 'fiddles'. Employment was also difficult to regulate and many foremen favoured relatives and friends. In the 19th and early 20th centuries, Welsh accents often predominated.

BONDED WAREHOUSES

Liverpool had a number of bonded warehouses – special buildings where goods could be stored without payment of import duties. The first examples, complete with special locks, were erected to house tobacco at King's Dock.

The five fireproof warehouse stacks surrounding Albert Dock (built 1846) each had substantial storage vaults. Built with cast iron frames, the stacks rose directly from the dock wall, the lower arcaded sections open at quayside level to ensure precious cargoes were transferred immediately into secure storage. At the rear were loading areas for onward transhipment by cart. The installation of hydraulic machinery would speed up the entire process.

Similar, if slightly more spartan, warehouses followed at Stanley and Wapping Docks.

This 1949 view highlights elements of the superstructure with its segmental brick arches and cast-iron columns, capitals and lintels supporting the mass of the brickwork. Note the wooden cradle slung above Bay B. Although the dock saw limited post-war use, bonded wine and spirits were stored here until 1972. In its heyday, hundreds of coopers once opened and repaired imported barrels for customs inspection. *G. H. Hesketh*

LEFT: Ongoing restoration work, instigated by the Merseyside Development Corporation in 1983, ensured that the docks complex, Grade One Listed and now a World Heritage Site, became a lasting legacy to the genius of its designer Jesse Hartley and to the works of Philip Hardwick and John Rennie. The clock tower was removed in the 1960s. *G. H. Hesketh*

BELOW: Although purely functional, the monumental Stanley Tobacco warehouse (1897-1901) is a potent reminder of Liverpool's trading links with the USA. Designed by A. G. Lyster, it has a staggering 27 million red and blue bricks on a steel and concrete frame. Thirteen storeys high, including basements for general storage, this bonded warehouse is 730 feet long and 125 feet high, and can store 65 million pounds of tobacco. During World War 2, its contents were valued at £40 million. Now part of the Stanley Conservation area, it is hoped that plans for its long-term preservation prove successful – although its low ceilings make it difficult to convert into apartments.

Visible in the foreground of the picture below are a pair of Hartley granite dock gates and a policeman's lodge. On the right is Hartley's South Warehouse (built 1854), isolated when the width of Stanley Dock was reduced to allow for construction of the tobacco warehouse. *Martin Jenkins, Online Transport Archive*

GRANARIES, SILOS AND REFINERIES

RIGHT: The Liverpool Grain Storage & Transit Company once owned several premises including the fortress-like Alexandra Warehouse, a combined granary and mill on Regent Road. Flexible pipes from overhead hoppers fed grain into waiting railway wagons and lorries. A Foden lorry can be seen waiting in the background. Seen passing in front shortly before its closure in 1965 is MD&HB No 36, one of a batch of four diesels delivered in 1959. *B. D. Pyne, Online Transport Archive*

BELOW: Grain reached the slab-like silos at Alexandra Dock after being sucked from ship's holds by a mix of fixed, travelling and floating grain elevators. Seen berthed in dock in 1974 are the Alexandra Towing Company tugs *Morpeth* (launched 1958, 193grt, formerly *West Cock*) and *Brocklebank* (1964, 173 grt). Today, the latter is an operational exhibit at the Maritime Museum. *J. G. Parkinson, Online Transport Archive*

TOP: Designed by G. F. Lyster, the three purpose-built, six-storey Waterloo Dock grain warehouses (1866-68) were then among the largest and most efficient in the world. Imported grain was raised directly from ships berthed alongside into the upper storeys by hydraulic elevators and conveyors, the machinery being housed in the tall brick turrets rising above roof-level. Inside, hydraulic machinery was utilised to sort, ventilate and store the grain that was discharged later for transport by road, rail or water. Changes included converting part of the complex into a mill in 1904 and adapting the east warehouse to handle oil seed in the 1920s. One block was demolished after war damage and the block on the left followed in 1969. Fortunately, the eastern block (right) survives as apartments.
J. G. Parkinson, Online Transport Archive

MIDDLE: Towering over Sefton Street on 23 May 1966 are contrasting silos on the east side of Coburg and Brunswick Docks, the newer (1936) concrete structure connected to the older (1906) brick counterpart by a high-level bridge. Both were demolished a year after closure, in 1988. A Leyland Comet and a Morris LD van are parked at the kerb, while the MD&HB diesel prepares to transfer a rake of wagons across the road into Brunswick goods station.
Peter J. Davies

BOTTOM: The only post-war warehouse of any architectural significance is the listed but now defunct Tate & Lyle Sugar Silo (1955-57) on Regent Road. This parabolic-arched, reinforced concrete structure (528 feet long x 87 feet high) was designed by the firm's engineering department to store 100,000 tons of raw sugar. Company lorries parked outside in 1964 made the transfer to the refinery on Love Lane. The high-level conveyor (now removed) connected with Huskisson Dock and bridged both the Dock Road and the Overhead Railway.
At Huskisson there were four grab cranes, each with a 'bite' of 2½ tons, to raise the raw sugar from the ships. MD&HB 0-6-0 No 40 was built by Hudswell Clarke in 1962.
Brian Faragher

II TRANSPORT

CANALS

Liverpool's status as 'second city of empire' depended on the ability of the Corporation and its merchants to improve and expand dock facilities, but also on effective transport links with the city's hinterlands. Coastal shipping accounted for a significant proportion of this and continued to do so well into the 20th century.

Initially, many of the developments in inland transport were in order to gain economic advantage. The first road out of Liverpool to be turnpiked, in 1729, led to collieries around Prescot, but also enabled the booming business of refining salt from Cheshire.

Similarly, the early 18th-century improvement of the rivers Irwell and Weaver, and the opening in 1757 of the first section of the Sankey Navigation, gave Liverpool local and regional advantages, much of it based on improving access to coal. But long-haul traffic into the interior was slow and inadequate. Almost all goods traffic in the early 18th century was by packhorse and, as late as 1750, the road to Warrington was unfit for coaches. In 1753, packhorses between Liverpool and London took nine days at an average of 23 miles per day. Even in the city itself roads were bad. An act of 1786 gave the Corporation powers to widen its streets at a time when there was not one wide or well-constructed street in Liverpool. The Corporation spent the then astonishing sum of £150,000 on improvements under the powers of the act.

The growth of a nationwide canal network allowed Liverpool's increasingly advantageous location for trade with Ireland and North America to be exploited to the full. For the first time, canals provided reliable inland transport for goods and there followed an era of roaring prosperity for the city and docks. With coal once more the initial stimulus, it led the Duke of Bridgewater to promote the canal that was to bear his name, opening in 1761 initially to take coal from his pits into Manchester, and later also to Runcorn and the Mersey tideway.

The 1760s also saw the authorising of the Trent & Mersey Canal, to run from the River Trent at Shardlow to the Runcorn Gap, and a junction with an extension of the Bridgewater. Its opening in 1777 represented the first step in connecting Liverpool to a national inland transport network that was both economical and reliable, also tapping into the industrial heartlands of the Midlands. From its earliest days it was also known as the Grand Trunk Canal, in the hope that other waterways would soon attach themselves to it as branches to a tree. Significantly, its chief advocate (besides the Staffordshire potter Josiah Wedgwood) was the Liverpool merchant Thomas Bentley, anticipating the widespread use of Liverpool capital to build the links on which the city's growth depended.

Liverpool still lacked a route eastwards into the industrial areas of Lancashire and Yorkshire, and to the North Sea. This led to the authorisation, in 1770, of what was to become the Leeds & Liverpool (L&L) Canal. Its construction would prove slow, although the section from Liverpool to Wigan was one of the first to be completed in 1777. The main line through to Leeds took until 1816, with a branch to join the Bridgewater at Leigh opening in 1820. At the Liverpool end, the L&L was later spanned by several road and rail bridges. Following the opening of Clarence Dock power station, power cables above the waterway were breached several times during World War 2. After the war, commercial usage slowly dried up so that, today, the surviving Liverpool sections are used solely by pleasure craft.

ABOVE: A barge belonging to Tate & Lyle is seen moored alongside the refinery in 1959, with Burlington Street bridge in the background. Now abandoned, this half-mile length south of the locks into Stanley Dock, once carried coal and other goods close to the city centre. *J. G. Parkinson, Online Transport Archive.*

LEFT: The Stanley cut (opened 1848), with its flight of four locks designed by J. B. Hartley, linked the L&L directly with the docks, although intended barge and rail docks were never built. Since 2009, pleasure craft using the flight are able to reach Albert Dock via a new link across the Pier Head. *J. G. Parkinson, Online Transport Archive*

RAILWAYS

The arrival of the railway transformed the city's fortunes. There are few moments in history that precisely divide past from future, or old from new; one such moment came shortly before eleven o'clock on Wednesday 15 September 1830, when George Stephenson stood on the footplate of the *Northumbrian*, ready to lead a procession of trains from Liverpool to Manchester, 30 miles away. Behind him was an eight-wheel triumphal carriage for the Duke of Wellington, then Prime Minister, and a four-wheeler for guests – one of whom, William Huskisson, MP for Liverpool, was cut down one hour later and killed by the locomotive *Rocket*.

The Liverpool & Manchester (L&M) was the world's first steam passenger railway, linking Liverpool, Europe's greatest Atlantic seaport, to Manchester, the world's first industrial city. It led to an immediate frenzy of railway building and a revolution in land transport. Within three months, 14 of the 26 road coaches running between Liverpool and Manchester had been withdrawn, even though the L&M ran only four trains a day and was suffering difficult teething problems. By 1832 only one road coach was left.

Apart from demonstrating beyond doubt the capabilities of the locomotive, the L&M also led the way in creating the administrative framework for the modern railway. It broke decisively with the practices of the turnpike roads and canals; it owned and worked the whole undertaking without subcontracting to other operators, employed a regular staff and established the scale of capital investment needed. It also led to the extensive involvement of Liverpool capital in the financing of railways all over England, during the railway mania of the 1840s.

But the railways did not have it all their own way. Although they had an advantage of price and speed when competing directly on stagecoach routes, elsewhere road traffic grew, feeding the burgeoning railway network with short-haul work. The number of horses on the roads, especially in Liverpool, increased dramatically as the effects of the railway combined to stimulate the economy, travel, trade and commerce. Even canals continued to compete with rail, at least initially, by cutting their rates so that, during the 1840s, the waterways between Liverpool and Manchester were still carrying more than twice the tonnage of the L&M.

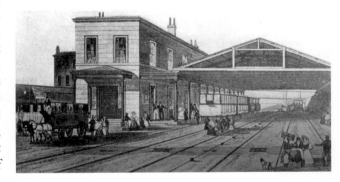

TOP RIGHT: The L&M's purpose-built passenger terminus at Crown Street was located outside the town centre, in a largely undeveloped area approached via a narrow tunnel (15 feet wide x 12 feet high) from Edge Hill. Soon, the two-storey station building, single platform and shed, spanning three tracks, proved inadequate. It would only be operational from 1830 to 1836.
Painting by Thomas Bury

RIGHT: One of the major civil engineering challenges to confront George Stephenson was Olive Mount cutting, which involved removing some 480,000 cubic yards of sandstone, some of which was used to construct the embankment at Roby and the Sankey Viaduct. Originally just over 20 feet wide and 70 feet deep, this rock chasm was one of the wonders of the age. It appeared less dramatic when widened to accommodate four tracks.
Martin Jenkins, Online Transport Archive

TOP: 'The Grand Area at Edge Hill' (as it was locally known) was rendered redundant when Lime Street station opened in 1836. The centre of L&M operations since 1830, it was here that the change took place from locomotive to rope haulage (see the foreground of the illustration). Dominating the rock cutting west of Chatsworth Way Bridge is the famous Moorish Arch, linking the two steam-winding engine houses with their 100-foot-tall chimneys. Today, some evidence still remains of these historic installations, as well as the tunnel to Crown Street. *Published by R. Ackerman, 1831*

MIDDLE: Opened in 1836, at the same time as the tunnel to Lime Street, Edge Hill is now the world's oldest passenger station still in regular use. All trains formerly stopped here before entering the tunnel; from this, the now largely obsolete Liverpool term 'getting off at Edge Hill' was coined as a euphemism for *coitus interruptus!* The station and the symmetrical retaining walls of the inclined approach roads are in red ashlar sandstone. In 1847, the L&NWR linked the buildings with an iron and glass roof, though this was removed in 1873. This historic station complex was returned to something like its original state in 1980, for the 150th anniversary celebrations of the L&M. *J. G. Parkinson, Online Transport Archive*

BOTTOM: The outer platforms at Edge Hill date from the widening of the tunnel down to Lime Street in the late 1880s. The spectacle of a steam locomotive, sometimes assisted by a banking engine, storming the grade up from Lime Street on London express trains, like the Red Rose and the Merseyside Express, was always exciting. Among legendary classes of locomotive that emerged at Edge Hill were Claughtons, Royal Scots, Patriots, Jubilees, Princess Royals and Princess Coronations, usually known as Duchesses. No 46206 was part of a small class of LMS-built 4-6-2 Pacifics, dating from 1935 and long associated with Liverpool-London services. *J. B. C. McCann, Online Transport Archive*

TOP: It was the inconvenient situation of Crown Street which led the L&M to cut the mile-long, steeply graded (maximum 1:83) tunnel through the sandstone from Edge Hill to its new station on Lime Street. After steam replaced cable haulage in 1870, much of the tunnel was opened up in 1881 to allow for smoke dispersal, which created an extraordinary cutting later widened by the L&NWR between 1885-90. This view shows the high bridges spanning the four tracks. *J. M. Ryan*

MIDDLE: The first Lime Street station with its monumental façade, designed by John Foster Junior, had a timber queen-post roof of 55-foot span. With the opening of the rail connection to Birmingham and London within two years and the subsequent growth in traffic, this was replaced by a new station built between 1846-51 to designs by William Tite, including a wider tunnel mouth and an iron segmental-arched roof of 153-foot six-inch span by Richard Turner (1798-1881), who designed the iron-and-glass palm house at Kew Gardens. It was then the widest single-span roof anywhere and marked a step forward in train-shed design.

Between 1867-71, the station was again rebuilt. Steam replaced cable, Foster's classical screen was demolished and the whole concourse redesigned. An enlarged train-shed with a curved, crescent-trussed roof of nearly 220-foot span resting on cast-iron columns was built to the designs of the L&NWR's engineer, William Baker (1817-78), and Francis Stevenson. In 1879 came a second span, designed by E. W. Ives.

This view is of the two 620-foot-long elliptical roofs before they were restored and re-glazed in 2001. All the buildings in front of the station, including the undistinguished tower block, have now gone. At its maximum extent, the station had 11 platforms with departures for most parts of the country. Over a million parcels a year were handled and there was even a bay for banana traffic from Garston Docks. *Mike Mercer*

BOTTOM: Under the chairmanship of Sir Richard Moon (1814-99), from 1861-91 the L&NWR, the world's largest joint-stock company, pursued an aggressive policy of expansion and innovation that quadrupled its share of Liverpool railway goods traffic between 1850-70. To overcome problems of movement to and from the docks, the company invested £2 million in redesigning existing facilities at Edge Hill. Part of the work took advantage of a natural slope to the west (see the middle of this picture) to create a vast marshalling yard with a gravity-operated gridiron. Each day, 80 or so men handled some 2,200 wagons on grades of 1:50 and 60 miles of track.

In this scene photographed on 24 November 1965, the green fireless locomotive (left) shunts the sidings serving Crawford's Biscuits, while the Stanier '8F' 2-8-0 has left the Crewe line and is using tracks which passed beneath the gridiron. Among the most complex railway sites in the world, the gridiron closed in 1982. Today, much of the site is occupied by Wavertree Technology Park. *B. Faragher*

Following opening of the L&M, the development of Liverpool's rail network was unlike that of other British cities. By the 1850s the town was already equal in size to Berlin and twice that of Brussels or Marseilles, so the role of the railway in its urban morphology was accordingly much less. The result was a geographically confusing network achieved at great cost and offering less than optimum convenience. But the role played by the railways in creating Liverpool's wealth cannot be overestimated. As the population approached 500,000 in the 1870s and the docks handled exports worth £55 million – more than in London – the L&NWR (which had succeeded the L&M) trumpeted the city's rapid expansion 'as one of the most remarkable instances of prosperity the world has seen'.

The magnet for the other companies was to share in the lucrative dock traffic and the transatlantic passenger trade; yet, despite the success of the L&M, it was 18 years before other railways arrived in the city. Serving areas to the north and east, these competing companies eventually came together as the Lancashire and Yorkshire Railway (L&Y) which built links into the docks. As passenger traffic increased, their first terminus at Great Howard Street (opened 1848) was replaced in 1850 by a new station at Tithebarn Street, later known as Exchange station and greatly expanded in a redesign by Henry Shelmerdine, with the approach tracks quadrupled.

The next major arrival was a consortium of the Great Northern, Manchester, Sheffield and Lincolnshire (renamed Great Central in 1897) and Midland Railways. In 1865/6 they formed the Cheshire Lines Committee (CLC), which offered a third passenger route to Manchester, initially from Brunswick (1864) and later Liverpool Central (1874), as well as giving each of the partners access to the docks via some heavily-engineered branch lines.

THE MERSEY RAILWAY

Standing today in the confines of James Street station, it is hard to imagine one of the Mersey Railway's (MR) powerful condensing locomotives bursting from the depths of the under-river tunnel after storming up its fierce gradient, still the steepest (1:27) on the present rail network. Hailed in 1886 as a major engineering achievement, the line from James Street, Liverpool to Green Lane, Birkenhead broke the monopoly of the Birkenhead ferries, although initially thousands deserted the acrid tunnel until electrification in 1903.

By 1892, the 4.5-mile network was complete with its subterranean terminus at Central Low Level. Electrified at 650v DC, the MR was the first in the UK to convert entirely from steam traction and to operate multiple-unit trains. Further innovations included automatic coloured-light signalling (1921), electro-pneumatic points and train-stops at Low Level (1923).

During the war, the under-river section never stopped running although James Street station was destroyed (as was that at Hamilton Square). Several generations of rolling stock have sparked through the high-arched, brick-lined tunnel. In 1977, Wirral Line services were re-routed onto a single-track, unidirectional tunnel with new stations connecting to mainline and Northern Line services. Gloomy Low Level was rebuilt and is now part of the Northern Line. In 1985, electric services through the tunnel were extended to Hooton and, subsequently, Chester (1993) and Ellesmere Port (1994).

With creation of the 'Big Four' in 1923, the L&NWR and L&Y (which had already merged in 1922) became part of the LMS, but the CLC remained jointly run: two

Seen here in 1966, a post-war Ivatt 2-MT Class 2-6-2T, No 41211, waits to leave Exchange with empty stock. The large train-shed comprised four gabled roofs supported at either end by solid brick walls. It was here that the last scheduled BR steam-hauled passenger train arrived on 3 August 1968. *Martin Jenkins, Online Transport Archive*

RIGHT: Exchange (1888-1977) had long associations with the electrified services to Southport and Ormskirk and, until its closure in 1951, the Aintree via Marsh Lane service. With the rapid growth in commuter traffic on the 18½-mile Southport line, it was electrified by the L&Y as early as 1904. After World War 2 traffic levels at Exchange declined, a situation made worse by the later transfer of long-distance services to Lime Street, so that in off-peak times the station sometimes possessed a ghostly silence with the stock waiting for the evening rush. For some 40 years, these EMUs first introduced by the LMS in 1939 were familiar on services to Southport and Ormskirk. *Marcus Eavis, Online Transport Archive*

BELOW: The scene below shows the three-storey station office block, complete with clock, that was the headquarters of the CLC, while the wooden canopy provided covered accommodation for traffic entering and leaving from Ranelagh Street. Behind it was a single-arch train-shed with six platforms. To the left of the Lyceum (right) was the entrance to the Central Low Level terminus of the Mersey Railway (MR). Behind was the original Lewis's store severely damaged during World War 2. *Commercial postcard, Martin Jenkins collection*

TOP: Despite having no access to Liverpool, the Great Western Railway was another major player. It achieved this by assuming joint ownership of the line from Chester to Birkenhead in 1860, enabling it to ferry goods across the river to and from four depots in Liverpool. It eventually handled some ten per cent of all rail freight passing through the port and was also one of the partners that, in 1857, promoted the bill to set up the MD&HB as a means of reconciling disputes between rival ports on either side of the Mersey. Here, an empty GWR lorry hurries past Bellamy-roof car 547 on its way to the GWR offices and warehouses at Manchester Basin. This was where the laden barges arrived from the Birkenhead side.
G. W. Price collection

LEFT: Original Mersey Railway steam-pumping stations survive in Birkenhead and on Mann Island, Liverpool. Now electrically-powered, the pumps still extract thousands of gallons of water from the tunnel. Today, the windowless building is isolated; everything around it, including Blake's Garage, has been demolished. Amazingly, two MR locomotives survive – including 0-6-4T No 5 *Cecil Raikes*, which was employed at Shipley Colleries until 1954 and is currently in long-term storage. Manchester Basin, used by GWR barges, was off to the far right and subsequently filled in.
A. S. Clayton,
Online Transport Archive

ABOVE: By the end of the 19th century, Liverpool's grip on the lucrative North Atlantic liner trade was increasingly threatened by Southampton, which was nearer to London and better equipped to handle larger vessels. None of Liverpool's terminal stations were convenient for direct access to the landing stage. To rectify this, the L&NWR and MD&HB introduced new arrangements in 1895. Locomotive haulage replaced cable on the branch to Waterloo Goods (opened 1849) and the MD&HB opened its two-platform Riverside Station on the landward side of the stage. Designed for rail-to-ship transfer, it was little more than a large transit shed with minimum

facilities. Used initially by boat trains, including the four-hour 'American Specials' from Euston which connected with Cunard and White Star ships, during both world wars the station was also used for troop movements. In fact, the very last departure, in February 1971, was a troop train from Northern Ireland.

When Riverside closed, it was no longer Southampton that was the issue but the decimation of liner services by competing airlines. The last sailings left the stage in 1972 and the site was subsequently cleared. *Commercial postcard, Martin Jenkins collection*

RIGHT: Fifteen minutes was the usual time taken to and from Edge Hill. Trains trundled at walking pace along the MD&HB tracks, with a flagman covering movements onto the Dock Road and a policeman into Waterloo Goods. Leaving Riverside was difficult with a heavy train and storming the Waterloo branch did, on occasion, require three steam locos. In 1949-50, the swing bridge across the entrance into Prince's Dock was strengthened and the tracks realigned to accommodate the weight of mainline locomotives. Controlling movements at the swing bridge was an unusual two-way signal – one for trains and one for ships. Seen here in 1968, clean 'Black Five' No 45305 crosses the bridge, heading a special train for enthusiasts into Riverside station.
A. S. Clayton, Online Transport Archive

ABOVE: In 1954, three of the L&NWR's 0-8-0s simmer close to the portal of Victoria Tunnel, the first of the two tunnels on the steeply-graded Waterloo Goods Branch. Introduced by the L&NWR in 1912, these powerful engines had long associations with Liverpool dock traffic, the last examples being withdrawn in 1962. Leading the trio is No 49082.

In classic stance, a policeman monitors the movements of a well-dressed photographer approaching Waterloo Tunnel Mouth's signal box. *J. B. C. McCann, Online Transport Archive*

BELOW: This photographic session on 13 June 1964 captured one of the four special six-wheeled brake vans marked 'Wapping Tunnel Working' (used to provide additional brake force on the steep descent), with 0-6-0 diesel-shunter No D3578 and a former L&Y 0-4-4T used as a stationary boiler for the nearby carriage sheds, in the background. *B. D. Pyne, Online Transport Archive*

thirds LNER, one third LMS. In 1948 the railways, including the MR, were nationalised, with the CLC becoming part of the Midland Region. As the docks declined, so passenger routes (including electric services) were withdrawn and stations closed. Following publication of the Beeching Report (1963) came the further closures of Birkenhead Woodside (1967), Liverpool Central High Level (1972) and Exchange (1977). More positively, between 1962-66 Liverpool Lime Street to London Euston was electrified and plans to close the electric service to Southport were sensibly dropped.

From 1971, the Merseyside Passenger Transport Authority, using the brand name Merseyrail, continued a process which resulted in 1977 in a radical reorganisation of most electric rail services. This facilitated the opening of new sections of underground tunnel known as 'The Loop', used by Wirral Line services, and 'The Link', used by the newly created Northern Line, extended to Garston in 1978 and to a main line interchange at Hunts Cross in 1983. Similar facilities existed in the tunnels at Moorfields, Lime Street and Central Station.

By 2010, some 35 years after the M53 on the Wirral linked into the new Mersey Tunnel (Kingsway, opened in 1971) and the trans-Pennine M62 connected the city to the M6 and Hull, Liverpool is at the hub of a network of electrified suburban services stretching as far as Chester and Crewe. Plans to electrify the historic route of the Liverpool and Manchester Railway now exist.

The next nine images below reflect a few aspects of the changing railway scene during the past 60 years.

TOP: Edge Hill (8A) was one of six post-war steam-locomotive power depots. It had all the usual facilities for handling anything from shunting to express locomotives including two substantial running sheds, repair sections, sheer legs, mechanical coaling stages, turntables and water-softening equipment. In 1966, part of the site was adapted to provide a diesel servicing area. This photograph, taken shortly before the end of steam in 1968, shows a driver and fireman who probably lived in the surrounding streets, preparing Stanier Class 5 4-6-0 No 45284 for duty. The site finally closed in 1983.
Martin Jenkins, Online Transport Archive

RIGHT: From the late 1950s, DMUs appeared in increasing numbers on British Rail. Here, the 11.07 from Wigan North Western to Liverpool Lime Street stops at Broad Green station on 18 October 1960. This Class 105 two-car set, from a batch built by Cravens of Sheffield between 1956-9, is in light green livery with cat's-whisker warning flashes and a characteristic upswept cant rail over the roof-mounted destination blind. In the late 1960s, the fast lines and associated buildings were removed to make way for the M62 link road. There has been a station at this location continuously since 1831. *Neil Cossons*

ABOVE: Three scenes, recorded in April 1968, show the former L&NWR Bootle branch (opened 1866) during the dying days of steam. With the gridiron in the background, a shabby 'Black Five' No 44692 takes a docks-bound mixed goods train through Edge Lane Junction. The box was destroyed by arsonists in the late 1980s. *Jerome McWatt, Online Transport Archive*

LEFT: On the slog up from Atlantic Junction, a hard-working goods train blasts out of Spellow tunnel and through the gloomy remains of Spellow station (1882-1948). Heavy freights still grumble up this gradient.
Martin Jenkins, Online Transport Archive

LEFT: After most services were diverted to Lime Street in 1966, an increasingly dingy Central station remained open until 1972, after which it was demolished. In 1959, Derby-built DMUs M79143 and M79656 are seen awaiting their next departures.
R. S. Stephens, Online Transport Archive

ABOVE: A freight from Brunswick passes through Cressington and Grassendale station in 1968. Four years later the station would close, but it was handsomely restored and reopened in 1978. *Martin Jenkins, Online Transport Archive*

RIGHT: With its many embankments and bridges, the heavily-engineered, now-defunct CLC North Liverpool extension (opened 1879), which fringed the city's eastern suburbs, provided access to Aintree Central (later Southport, 1884) and the docks stations (1880). Seen in 1970, a DMU waits to leave Gateacre for Liverpool Central, all regular passengers services north of this point having closed in 1960. *Jerome McWatt, Online Transport Archive*

ABOVE: Among the North Liverpool extension stations closed was West Derby, where No 42112, a post-war Fairburn 2-6-4 tank, is seen pausing in February 1960 with the Saturdays-only 13.12 Gateacre to Aintree Central. Ostensibly operated for those still working a five-and-a-half-day week, by this time overstaffed stations like this were often devoid of passengers.
After scheduled passenger traffic ended, the line was used by Grand National specials until 1963. *Neil Cossons*

BELOW: Along with scores of loss-making passenger services, BR also closed hundreds of goods yards during the 1960s as domestic coal deliveries declined and pick-up freights were withdrawn. Those on the north extension fizzled out during a ten-year period, with West Derby going early in June 1964. This 1959 view shows a double-arm/double-direction signal. The line closed in 1978, with the end of freight operations at Huskisson goods station. Since 2001, the track bed has formed part of Cycleway Network Route 62, Trans-Pennine Trail. *Neil Cossons*

RAILWAY HOTELS

RIGHT: The most famous hotel in the city is the Adelphi. In fact, three hotels with the same name have stood on the same site, the first dating from 1826 and the second from 1876. When the latter was acquired by the Midland Railway in 1892, it was decided to replace it with 'the finest hotel outside of London'. This was the third Adelphi, designed by Frank Atkinson (1871-1923) who had been articled to a Liverpool architect before setting up on his own account in London. It was in 1907 that he collaborated with Daniel H. Burnham, the Chicagoan designer of the new steel-framed Selfridge's store on Oxford Street. The low-relief exterior and almost flush windows of the Adelphi reflect this influence, with a thin Portland stone skin hung on a steel space frame.

Kept from completion by the outbreak of World War 1, the design was never fulfilled. But for generations of travellers it remained a first-class railway hotel, its clean modern lines exuding an air of opulence and sophistication. Passengers arriving by rail stayed overnight before embarking from the landing stage. Countless celebrities have stayed here during Grand National week, the Adelphi's afternoon teas were a cherished local attraction and it has even starred in its own fly-on-the-wall TV series. Although some original features have been removed, the Britannia Adelphi, as it is now called, remains in business. *Clive Garner collection*

LEFT: Designed by Alfred Waterhouse, the opulent 300-bedroom North Western Hotel (opened 1871) was built by the L&NWR to be the best in the city at the time of its opening. Its French Renaissance style contrasted aggressively with St George's Hall and the strong classical themes already permeating the William Brown Street area opposite. Statesmen, politicians and stars of stage and screen all spent time in its opulent lounges and restaurants, en route to the New World. On closure in 1933, the building was used as railway offices and renamed Lime Street Chambers, the LMS redirecting its hotel customers to the Adelphi and the Exchange. Since 1997, it has served as student accommodation for John Moores University.

It is seen in its heyday of 1891, when horse traffic was dominant. To the immediate north of the hotel is the Alexandra Theatre (later the Empire) and the 132-foot column (built 1863) in memory of the Duke of Wellington.
F. Frith, Martin Jenkins, David Packer and Jerome McWatt, Online Transport Archive

ABOVE: The Exchange Hotel was incorporated into the new Exchange station (built 1886-8), designed by Henry Shelmerdine (1865-1935) and fronting onto Tithebarn Street. Built in the favoured extempore Renaissance style of the time, it had 150 bedrooms, a banqueting hall, a ballroom and a canopied entrance to the west of the twin arches into the station itself, where there was a bust of John Pearson (1824-87), Chairman of the L&Y and a Mayor of Liverpool, and an impressive three-faced clock. The keystones carry the heads of the Prince of Wales (later Edward VII) and Princess Alexandra. When the station closed in 1977, the decision was taken to retain and restore the frontage which now forms the façade of the Mercury Court office development, dating from the mid-1980s. *A. S. Clayton, Online Transport Archive*

ROAD TUNNELS

Liverpool's capacity for innovation continued even in the darkest days of economic depression. On occasion, it even resulted from them. The building of the first Mersey road tunnel (Queensway, 1934) was in part to relieve chronic post-war unemployment. Constructed by engineers J. A. Brodie, B. Hewett and B. Mott, the 2.1-mile tunnel with its two branches of 0.8 miles was at the time the longest in the world to run underwater. Costing £7 million, it was rightly praised as 'an exemplary engineering achievement'. A drive through the sinuous four-lane main tunnel remains an exhilarating experience. *Clive Garner collection*

ABOVE: Herbert J. Rowse, architect to the Mersey Tunnel Joint Committee, designed the Portland stone and brick ventilation shafts, the tunnel entrances, the startling art deco-style tollbooths and 'shafts of light' at each main entrance. Reconstructed after war damage, the giant George's Dock Ventilation and Control Room (opened 1934), is seen here in 1961. Housing the tunnel offices and controlling air quality in the tunnel, its various panels and statues appropriately represent Night and Day, Speed, Civil Engineering, Architecture and Construction. The still open, but almost deserted, South docks, can be seen stretching into the distance towards the two grain silos on Sefton Street. *Tom Parkinson, Online Transport Archive*

ABOVE: Construction of the twin-bore Kingsway tunnel (1971) and its approaches led to mass demolition, especially in the Scotland Road area. Both tunnels are now used by a network of cross-river bus routes, some in direct competition with ferry and rail services. To the left are examples of different Liverpool Corporation flats and, in the foreground, locally produced Ford Anglia cars and a 'wagon and drag' lorry. Tolls are charged and the tunnels also have their own dedicated police force. In the 1950s, Dinky Toys produced a model of one of their vehicles. *J. M. Ryan*

TRAMS AND BUSES

The core of the Liverpool tram system evolved during the horse era. Following an unsuccessful experiment in 1861, construction began in earnest in 1869. In 1897, the Corporation purchased the Liverpool Tramways & Omnibus Company for £567,000, with electrification occurring rapidly between 1898 and 1901; the last horse-drawn tram operated in Litherland in 1903.

Nearly all routes converged on the Pier Head, although to disperse the load other city centre termini were used as 'workers' rush hour queue points', or for boarding football and race cars. Cheap fares encouraged greater mobility for work, shopping, entertainment and leisure. Early morning workmen's returns, free transfers between certain routes and a child's 1d-return in the school holidays all survived until 1957. Service levels were frequent, especially at peak times, with several routes often covering key transport corridors. 'Industrial services' catered for labour-intensive areas such as Seaforth, Edge Lane, Gillmoss and Kirkby. From the city centre, the dense network fanned out into the old inner city districts, often tackling steep gradients before reaching the northern, eastern and southern suburbs.

Between 1908 and 1923, Liverpool was the only British city to run first-class cars on selected services. It also opened the first stretch of segregated grass track in September 1914. Having proved successful, many more miles were built into the developing suburbs and, where practical, existing lines were relocated onto grass tracks. The final stretch opened between 1942-4, carrying some of the 20,000 people employed at the Royal Ordnance Factory at Kirkby. Looking to the future, consideration was given to tram subways and coupled pairs of modern single-deckers, but these exciting concepts were dropped. By 1945, the worn-out system was plagued by power cuts, breakdowns, car shortages and the threat of increased electricity costs. It was also under attack from 'modernists' who argued that trams would hinder post-war renewal. The decision was taken to convert the 97-mile system to buses, the process completed on 14 September 1957 when the last of the 744 trams were replaced.

A couple of laden company horse trams with knifeboard upper-deck seating head up Lord Street towards the Pier Head. Each car has had an additional 'trace horse' added in order to tackle the steep gradient. In 1886, only inbound trams used Lord Street. Much of the south side was later destroyed during World War 2. Today's survivors from the horse age include a tram, the façade of an omnibus depot and a short length of track.
F. Frith, Martin Jenkins, David Packer, Jerome McWatt, Online Transport Archive

ABOVE: The first electric terminus was outside St George's Church on South Castle Street. From 1898-1901, the A (Dingle) was operated by 15 sets of German-built four-wheel motorcars and trailers, most of which were later scrapped – although some did survive, including trailer 429, the subject of a failed preservation attempt in the 1950s.

Assigned to the B (Prince's Park Gates) in 1899 were 15 centre-entrance bogie cars imported from the USA, most of which lasted into the 1920s, although three were converted into vast open-toppers nicknamed 'Olympics' and were in use until 1933. After these early imports, scores of conventional four-wheel double-deckers were either purchased or built at the Corporation's Lambeth Road works; some types or features carried the name of a General Manager – for example, Bellamy (roof), Mallins (balcony), Priestly (standard four wheel tram) and Marks (modern bogie car).

Note the early fire ladder, the ornate electric light standards, the sweep of St George's Crescent (destroyed in 1941) and the range of headgear – especially the city gent sporting his topper and frock coat. *Merseyside Fire Brigade*

BELOW: The Liverpool system had examples of single and interlaced track usually dictated by narrow streets. This interlaced section on Beloe Street, Dingle lasted from 1935 to 1951. Car 919 (later sold to Glasgow) passes a row of grimy terraced houses with steps up to the front doors and entrances into cellars and basements, where coal deliveries were often dumped outside on the pavement. The iron railings seem to have escaped the wartime scrap drive. *A. S. Clayton, Online Transport Archive*

LEFT: Designed to produce 1,000 trams, Edge Lane Works (1928-1997), the largest UK municipal factory of its kind, had a range of shops employing nearly 1,000 men, a tram depot and motorbus facilities. Over the years it built some 460 trams, including 270 bogie cars between 1931 and 1937. When a green livery was introduced in 1933, new cars were nicknamed 'Green Goddess' after a contemporary movie. Edge Lane also rebuilt older trams and assembled scores of bus bodies but, as construction techniques improved, by the 1980s it was no longer cost-effective and the site was cleared shortly after closure.

These bogie streamliners are under construction in the late 1930s. In one of those fascinating little quirks of history, the works did not build the city's last new tram, a railgrinder which emerged from the workshop of the City Engineers in 1948. *Martin Jenkins collection*

BELOW: During the bombing of August 1940 to May 1941, 2,700 people were killed, thousands of homes destroyed or damaged, churches, schools and hospitals obliterated. At this time, the trams were sometimes restricted to the fringes of the central district.

When this view was photographed, buildings on the south side of Lord Street had largely been cleared, petrol rationing was restricting car usage, the Victoria Monument (built 1904) was unscathed and the trams still had wartime white bumpers and headlamp masks. *Martin Jenkins collection, Online Transport Archive*

TOP: The brainchild of City Engineer J. A. Brodie, the pioneering grass tracks were part of the Corporation's interwar policy of relocating people into new 'garden suburbs'. Quality municipal housing would be served by segregated tramway reservations, mostly laid in the centre of spacious, well-designed dual carriageways flanked by neat privet hedges. One of the 163 bogie streamliners (built 1936-7) is seen standing at Utting Avenue East terminus in 1955. Built to budget, these fast, stylish 78-seat 'liners' soon developed structural problems. Despite this, 46 were sold to Glasgow in 1953-4, the last examples being withdrawn in 1960 – only one of which is now preserved.
By the early 1950s, the remnants of the system had recovered from wartime deprivations and rebuilt 'liners', unimpeded by older cars with slower motors, really showed their paces on the miles of re-laid track. *Ray DeGroote, Online Transport Archive*

RIGHT: On 8 September 1957, car 245 carried enthusiasts for a farewell tour of the final routes. Now preserved, 245 was one of a group of 100 four-wheel 'baby grands' built at Edge Lane between 1938-42. This roundabout on Edge Lane was unusual in that trams ran around it rather than through the middle. The junction has since been totally remodelled and the flats in the background demolished. *W. G. S. Hyde, Online Transport Archive*

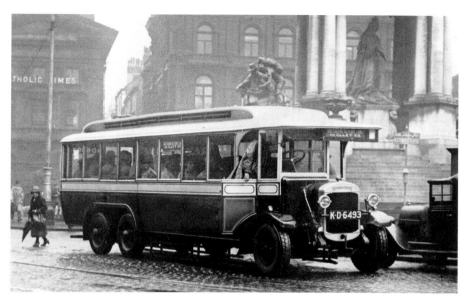

TOP: From humble beginnings in 1911, Corporation buses gradually operated tram-feeder services and much-needed outer suburban links. The Pier Head was reached in 1928, but by 1939 there were still only 158 buses. During the war, second-hand vehicles had to be utilised; between 1946-51, 500 double-deckers were acquired mostly as tram replacements. Built to Corporation specifications, Liverpool buses had a somewhat utilitarian reputation and were dismissed by some as 'spam-cans' during the 1950s.

In 1963, Liverpool took delivery of the first of 380 rear-engined Leyland Atlanteans; they were followed in 1968 by the first of a number of one-man single-deckers. In 1969, Liverpool merged with Birkenhead and Wallasey to form the Merseyside Passenger Transport Executive (MPTE), and Cross River Express buses began running through the second Mersey road tunnel in 1971, the success of which led to the opening of more cross-river services through both tunnels. In 1986 the MPTE, which now included Southport and St Helens, was finally disbanded due to deregulation. This led to service contractions and the closure of long-established garages, some being former tram depots. The variety of early buses had ranged from small petrol electrics to big six-wheel Karriers and Thorneycrofts. *Martin Jenkins collection, Online Transport Archive*

MIDDLE: Liverpool's long association with AEC started in 1935, with delivery of the company's first Regent double-deckers, a total of 172 entering service by 1940. More Regents featured in the tram replacement orders which also included Crossleys, Daimlers and Leylands. Many bodies, built by several manufacturers, were assembled or completed at Edge Lane works. *Martin Jenkins collection, Online Transport Archive*

BOTTOM: The first eight-foot-wide buses were delivered in 1951 and the last traditional rear-loaders in 1961. On 10 May 1956, a badly parked Hillman Minx prevented rush-hour buses, some on tram replacement routes, from loading at the staggered kerbside stops on Renshaw Street, a main transport corridor to the south. *Martin Jenkins collection*

RIGHT: Trade-union opposition to higher capacity vehicles delayed the entry into service of the first rear-engined Leyland Atlanteans until 1963. Eventually, over 380 were delivered, but once again there was opposition when they were converted to one-man operation. The poorly-designed Pier Head bus station lasted from 1965-1991. *Marcus Eavis, Online Transport Archive*

BELOW: Crosville and Ribble both provided intensive services to parts of the city, while other operators included Lancashire United and St Helens and Wigan Corporations. Ribble jointly operated the 50-series routes into the northern suburbs with the Corporation. Here, buses belonging to both operators are seen at the Old Haymarket. This view highlights the art deco lamp standards and the 60-foot tall 'shaft of light', clad in fluted and polished black granite. Although this one has disappeared, the Birkenhead column survives. *G. H. Hesketh*

In 2011, Liverpool's transport web continues to evolve. Bus deregulation has not delivered hoped-for results; full integration of road and rail services seems as far away as ever. In general planning terms, the city has recovered from its love affair with the car, as exemplified by the flyovers into the north end of Dale Street and Tithebarn Street, although housing on Edge Lane is blighted in advance of the extension of the M62 into the central area.

After World War 2, redevelopment plans included overspill towns and estates (many built) and an inner ring road which fulfilled contemporary demand (by some) for high-speed car movements. Then, for a while, the city embraced an ambitious plan submitted in 1965 by their planning consultants, Shankland Cox, which, had it been adopted, would have brought radical and irrevocable change to the central areas of the city as a result of major road development springing from an inner ring road and attendant feeders. Vigorously and successfully opposed, Shankland disappeared, but not before some damage had been done. In the words of the late novelist Beryl Bainbridge, 'Someone's murdered Liverpool and got away with it.'

'The City of Change and Challenge' (as Liverpool was described by its municipal 1960s slogan) is symbolised today by St John's Precinct and its massive 450-foot beacon. Although much knocked around, key elements survive but today Liverpool would benefit from the planning equivalent of the dynamic vision and imagination shown in the interwar years, when well-designed estates were served by effective public transport.

In 2010, an inspired plan for reintroducing trams as a key element of the city's regeneration programme seems to have been thwarted by complicated arguments over funding. On the positive side, John Lennon Airport serves an increasing number of destinations; much of the local rail network is electrified; the two road tunnels provide good links with Liverpool's hinterland and fast trains to Euston take little over two hours.

Appropriately, it was from Liverpool that the '15-guinea special', the last scheduled steam passenger working on BR departed on 11 August 1968, reviving memories of that supremely important moment 138 years earlier when the railway as we know it was born.

SPEKE AIRPORT

The renowned aviator Sir Alan Cobham (1894-1973) campaigned in the late 1920s for a network of municipal airports to be built across Britain. Supported by the Liverpudlian Viscount Wakefield (1859-1941), creator of the Castrol oil empire, in 1928 Liverpool City Council bought the estate of Speke Hall on the north bank of the Mersey estuary, one of the finest Tudor manor houses in Britain, and 418 acres were set aside for an airport. By 1939 some 40 airports had been built, but Speke was unique as an exemplar of best practice and for the quality of its architectural design and construction.

The new airport was designed in art deco style by Edward Bloomfield in the Liverpool City Surveyor's department, drawing his inspiration from Hamburg's 1929 terminal building at Fuhlsbüttel. Construction began in 1935. Hangar No 1 and the control tower were opened in July 1937, to be followed by the rest of the terminal building and Hangar No 2 to the east. The whole architectural ensemble is still complete although no longer in use for aviation, having been replaced by the new John Lennon Airport officially opened by Yoko Ono in 2002. Today, the Speke terminal – now a hotel – stands with Tempelhof, Berlin and Le Bourget, Paris as one of the finest and most complete survivors of the 1930s' purpose-built European airports. This 1958 scene features a British European Airways DC3. *Liverpool Public Record Office*

III INDUSTRY

Little evidence remains of Liverpool's earliest industries such as watch-making, pottery, shipbuilding, salt refining, printing, whaling and fishing. As the Dock Estate expanded, a range of new industries were established. These were mostly concerned with processing bulk imports such as grain, oil seed, rubber, sugar, timber and non-ferrous metals. There was also a group of interconnected secondary industries – for example, biscuits and sweets relying on sugar and flour, timber for matches and electrical cables needing copper and rubber. Even white-collar industries such as banking, broking, the futures market and insurance relied on the port's maritime base. The main ongoing problem was the lack of any real manufacturing base independent of the port and the river. This overriding dependence on sea transport meant that Liverpool was putting all its eggs in one basket – and allowing central government to hold the basket.

Matters came to a head after World War 1, when male unemployment levels were consistently above 20 per cent and some 60,000 a day were looking for casual work in the docks. The situation worsened following the Great Depression of 1929, with 44 per cent of the population living below or just above the poverty line. With vivid memories of a transport strike (1911)and a chaotic police strike (1919), fears grew that the city would again face savage industrial unrest.

In 1936, the city council obtained powers to build and finance a series of industrial estates which were gradually established at Speke, Aintree, Kirkby and Knowsley. The former, the first to be built, was a self-contained entity with a mix of houses for managers and workers built close to new industrial premises. In 1939 the industrial section was well advanced, but the houses were not completed until 1954. As part of the rearmament drive, Rootes established an airframe plant at Speke (occupied post war by Dunlop's). Royal Ordnance Factories (RFOs) were opened at Kirkby and Fazakerley and a Napier aircraft engine works at Gillmoss. At the end of the war, the Corporation acquired these sites for development as industrial estates which eventually employed some 80,000. Farmland purchased from Lancashire County Council was used for overspill housing and for resale to firms like ICI on which to build factories.

Post-war efforts aimed at resolving the city's chronic unemployment problem started in the 1950s, with government incentives to encourage companies to open factories in Liverpool, many of which offered women fulltime work for the first time. A second wave of investment followed in the 1960s, when generous government grants led to the opening of two car plants at Halewood (Ford) and Speke (Standard-Triumph). Including those at the Vauxhall plant at Ellesmere Port, 30,000 jobs were created on Merseyside and for a period the dream of full employment seemed to be a reality.

Things rapidly turned sour. Following strikes and mass job losses, the MD&HB collapsed with debts of £90 million. Then the mid-1970s global recession and oil crisis crippled the recently established manufacturing base. Between 1971-84, over 450 factories closed with the loss of some 100,000 jobs. The much-heralded post-war diversification had indeed brought industry to Liverpool, but many of its branch factories were vulnerable to the first signs of economic downturn.

The city's plight was highlighted in *The Boys from the*

Black Stuff, Alan Bleasdale's TV drama with its haunting refrain of 'gissa job'. For many former dock workers, the change from the culture of 'casualism' to the regimentation of the production line proved difficult. Many also perceived an 'anti-Scouse' attitude from management, while the media tended to focus on militant labour relations and crippling strikes, with any coverage of the city featuring depressing images of dereliction and vandalism. Jobs also disappeared in the service industries, with offices, shops and firms boarded up until some 15 per cent of land was derelict or vacant.

The population also continued to decline as many left the city or were rehoused. At the time of the Toxteth riots of 1981, Liverpool seemed to be on the brink. During the 1980s there was evidence of some regeneration as well as a revival in seaborne trade, but employment only started to improve in 1993 when the EU recognised Liverpool's exceptional circumstances, granting it Objective One status for regeneration. Matters further improved when the city secured the Capital of Culture title (for the year 2008) in 2003 and was designated a UNESCO World Heritage Site in 2004, both of which helped to develop a new tourist industry. Business parks were also created to further boost employment. Today, the main employers are the government, the city council and the three universities.

Many of the factories on the Speke Industrial Estate have been demolished. Dunlop's (formerly Rootes) is now occupied by long-term airport car parks. However, this Grade I art deco factory (opened 1919) on Speke Boulevard, acquired by Bryant & May in 1929, has been converted into the Matchworks office complex by developers Urban Splash, with a view to the Speke-Garston Partnership attracting new business into the area. For years, famous brands like Swan, Pilot, Vesta and England's Glory were manufactured there from wood imported through Garston Docks. Once the largest match factory in Britain and second largest in Europe, it was latterly the only producer of wooden matches before it closed in 1994. *John Collingwood*

TOP, MIDDLE AND BELOW: Parts of Kirkby Trading Estate still function today. Opened in 1939 as Royal Ordnance Factory (ROF) No 7, it was purchased after the war by the Corporation who transformed it into a trading estate which, by 1971, employed 26,000 people. These three photographs were taken in November 1956, shortly after replacement of the Kirkby tram services when 31 redundant cars met a fiery end on the estate.

Car 153 was on track opened as late as 1944. To the left was Kirkby Main Gate, served by many additional buses and trams during rush hours.

On the length of tramway between Main Gate and No 5 Gate was a crossing with part of the extensive Corporation-owned, internal, estate railway (1943-1976). Car 889 is being manoeuvred from one track to the other. During the war, thousands used a passenger station built on the west side of the ROF.

Despite calls for trams to be reinstated due to the fuel shortage caused by the Suez crisis, they were towed a quarter of a mile to some disused meat sidings by one of a pair of diesel-mechanical Vulcan Drewry 0-6-0s delivered in 1954, each of which had vacuum brakes to handle special tank wagons. This is City of Liverpool No 4. Various wartime units can be seen in the background.
G. C. Bird,
Online Transport Archive

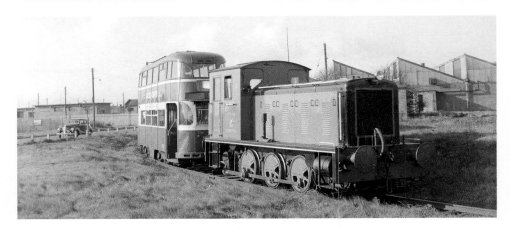

LEFT: Tate & Lyle (T&L) was a local industrial giant. In 1869, the self-made Unitarian businessman Henry Tate founded a refinery on Love Lane, Vauxhall, for the production of sugar cubes. Following several mergers and acquisitions, including Lyle's in 1921, T&L was ultimately responsible for 60 per cent of Britain's sugar supplies. Among local industries relying on the refinery were Barker & Dobson (confectionery), Crawford's and Jacob's (biscuits) and W. P. Hartley (jam). Changing trade patterns, and the concentration on sugar beet following Britain's membership of the EEC, led T&L to cut its losses and pull out of Liverpool in 1981, with the loss of 1,500 jobs in Vauxhall, an area with 46 per cent unemployment. Church leaders and politicians joined shop stewards and T&L workers in the fight to save jobs but, as with similar actions at United Biscuits, Dunlop, Fisher-Bendix, Lucas-CAV and GEC-AIE-EE, it was all to no avail. T&L's closure came to symbolise the city's economic decline. In the harsh world of profit, there was no empathy for a family firm which maintained excellent labour relations. Following strong local pressure, the T&L site was redeveloped as the Eldonian Village between 1987-95. *J. G. Parkinson, Online Transport Archive*

RIGHT: Some older Liverpudlians may recall this pair of Venetian-style walkways (nicknamed Ponti della Succari, or 'Bridges of Sugar'), linking two sections of the T&L refinery on Vauxhall Road. From here granulated, caster, pulverised and mineral water sugar was despatched around the country, together with cake icing, golden syrup and treacle. Seen here in 1949, a standard four-wheel tram heads for town on Route 16. *N. N. Forbes*

LEFT: One of the firms to purchase molasses from T&L was J. Bibby & Sons, whose warehouse complex of vegetable and animal oil mills was one of the largest in the world. When founded in Liverpool in 1885, production was confined to seed-crushing and cattle feed (eventually producing 10,000 tons a week). Later, the production of soap, paper, edible oils and fats created an array of pungent smells. Located close to the grain warehouses at Waterloo Dock, the site was demolished in the late 1980s. Known for its progressive labour relations, with its 3,000 employees subscribing to pension schemes and benefiting from a five-day week, Bibby's was sold to Prince's and later became part of Associated British Foods. *J. G. Parkinson, Online Transport Archive*

TOP: Thousands of boys (and men) were devoted to the high-quality products of the Meccano factory on Binns Road (1914-1979), off Edge Lane. Inspired by Frank Hornby, a dedicated workforce produced Meccano (established 1907), Hornby trains (1920) and Dinky toys (1931). In 1964, Dinky was taken over by Lines Bros (Tri-ang), who went into liquidation in 1971 when Meccano Ltd was bought by Airfix. At its peak, the factory employed over 1,000 (mostly women), who were ultimately let down by the company's poor investment and failure to tackle aggressive competition. *Liverpool Public Record Office*

MIDDLE: An all too common sight – the famous factory is boarded up. Special industrial tram and bus services once catered for this and other nearby factories, including Automated Telephone, Crawford's Biscuits and Littlewoods. *Alan Atkinson*

BOTTOM: Two major English biscuit manufacturers, Crawford's and W&R Jacobs, both had Liverpool factories that relied upon supplies from Tate & Lyle. Part of United Biscuits since 1962, parts of Crawford's factory (built 1897) on Binns Road are still operational, although a Grade 11 listed section was demolished in the 1980s. Another firm with good labour relations, it provided women with a viable alternative to domestic service. Seen in 1964, Crawford's fireless locomotive *Dolly May* (1917) shunts wagons on the company's private siding which connected the factory to the mainline. *Brian Faragher*

LEFT: Today, the pools giants are still major employers and rely heavily on cheaper female labour. Vernon's began running football pools from its Liverpool base in 1925. Part of Ladbroke's since 1989, it now also focuses on lottery games via the internet and telephone. *Photographer unknown*

BELOW: Utilising imported tobacco, several cigarette manufacturing firms opened in Liverpool, including Ogden's. From humble beginnings, it opened this impressive factory on Boundary Lane in 1899, soon to produce 900 million cigarettes a year! The factory also manufactured snuff, St Bruno and St Julien pipe tobacco and packaged Golden Virginia rolling tobacco. From 1902, it became part of Imperial Tobacco. After closure a few years ago, permission was refused to demolish the Grade II listed factory. *Neil Cossons*

IV ARCHITECTURE AND HOUSING

*' ... one of the neatest, best built towns
I have seen in England.'*

*'. . . at the top of the court stand the
open cesspit and privy.'*

From the beginning of the 18th century, the city's distinctive urban landscape, the scale and quality of its buildings, had become an increasing source of wonder and amazement. Reflecting on her travels throughout England, Celia Fiennes (1662-1741) saw Liverpool as early as 1698 as, 'a very Rich trading town, ye houses of Brick and stone built high and Even ... it's London in miniature as much as ever I saw.' Her contemporary, Daniel Defoe (*c*1659-1731), said in 1724, 'There is no town in England, London excepted, that can equal Liverpool for the fineness of the streets, the beauty of the buildings; many of the houses are all of stone and the rest (the new part) of brick.' In 1755, John Wesley (1703-91) noted, 'Liverpool, one of the neatest, best built towns I have seen in England.'

By the second half of the 19th century, it was not just the scale and magnificence of the Dock Estate but the expression of mercantile wealth reflected in great buildings, commercial and civic, that made Liverpool a place of such extraordinary architectural eminence. In the process, older structures, established industries and admired beaches were ruthlessly swept aside to make way for new buildings of elegance and style, ranging from John Wood's magnificent Liverpool Town Hall, completed in 1754, to the Bank of England on Castle Street (1845-8) and St George's Hall (1854), all of which gave the city a visible stature that matched her emerging role as gateway to the world. In the heart of Liverpool, all within a half-hour's walk, could be found every element of the banking, commercial, ship-owning, cargo-handling and marine insurance communities that made the city tick.

Not everyone responded favourably to the utilitarian buildings of the waterfront – although the observations of Sir J. A. Picton, town councillor, historian and campaigner for public libraries, need to be seen in the context of his also being an architect and later President (1876-7) of the Liverpool Architectural Society. The Picton Library – one of the outstanding group of buildings on William Brown Street which, with the museum and the Walker Art Gallery, forms Liverpool's cultural nucleus – is named after him. He wrote in 1873 of Albert Dock, 'The works for strength and durability are unsurpassable, but it is to be regretted that no attention whatever has been paid to beauty as well as strength. The enormous pile of warehouses which looms so large upon the river ... is simply a hideous pile of naked brickwork.' Popular revulsion at the severity of these and other industrial buildings prevailed for nearly a century, before a new generation, seeing them through new eyes, recognised that in the functional elegance of their austere design lay a new architectural and engineering idiom: the roots of the modernist movement.

The Edwardian years represented high noon in the fortunes of Liverpool as a city distinguished by the majesty of its great buildings. Central to this was the waterfront and the bravura statement of the three Pier Head buildings, each spectacular in its own right but, when seen together, forming one of the most striking and unforgettable frontages in the world. The site was created in 1899, when the Corporation decided to drain the outdated George's

Dock. First to be built were the new offices for the MD&HB (1907), followed by the Royal Liver Friendly Society's headquarters, the Liver Building (1911), and, between the two, the Cunard Building (1916). Conceived quite consciously as landmarks, they instantly came to symbolise Liverpool at the height of its self-confidence. In the words of Nikolaus Pevsner, they 'represent the great Edwardian Imperial optimism and might indeed stand at Durban or Hong Kong just as naturally as at Liverpool.'

In the years down to World War 2, buildings of an indigenous Liverpool style were to give parts of the city a conspicuously North American flavour. Some of these were the work of Liverpool architects, especially those trained in the new School of Architecture at the University. One such, Herbert J. Rowse (1887-1963), who was born in Crosby and graduated from Liverpool in 1907, was to become the city's most influential architect of the interwar years. Others exerted their influence all over the world, from Palestine to South Africa, Canada to Zanzibar, through what came to be known as the 'Liverpool Manner', a term coined to describe the school's particular brand of classicism.

Much of Liverpool's long tradition of council housing was also of groundbreaking and distinguished design. One survivor, St Andrew's Gardens (1934-35), designed by Liverpool graduate John Hughes (1903-77), was much admired by Walter Gropius, who visited the city and taught briefly in the School of Architecture.

Designed by Walter Thomas, the much-admired Philharmonic Hotel (opened 1900) on Hope Street highlights the extraordinary decorative work undertaken by students from Liverpool's School of Architecture (initially also including Applied Arts). Admitting its first students in 1895 under Roscoe Professor of Architecture Frederick Moore Simpson (1855-1928), the school rapidly developed a reputation for free-thinking originality. Simpson's own sympathies stemmed from the city's long classical tradition, rooted in the predilections of non-conformist merchant princes like William Roscoe, the Rathbones and the Holts, and outstanding buildings like Elmes's St George's Hall, 'Europe's finest neo-classical building.' Simpson was also an admirer of American architectural teaching, especially the course at Columbia University, so that by the time he was succeeded by Charles Herbert Reilly (1874-1948) in 1904, a theme had been established that was to pervade the school's work and the professional influence of its graduates. *Neil Cossons*

The years after World War 2 found a city in which the wealth of its glory days had largely evaporated, faced with making good after the destruction of the Blitz and the backlog of housing renewal against the context of a declining population and low per-capita income. As a result thousands of substandard houses were demolished, although much of the new building (including the notorious tower blocks) of the last half-century has been poor in design and construction, made all the more apparent by the contrast with the legacy of the city's distinguished past.

One of the effects of the decline in population has been the creation of more space in the former Victorian heartlands than can now be effectively used. This has had some curious results. Areas once packed with high-density slums (and then with 1960s tower blocks) are now occupied by low-rise housing in neat suburban style, grouped in closes and cul-de-sacs. Today, Thomas Duncan's great 1857 water tower on the heights of Everton, a commanding and expressive symbol of Liverpool's 19th-century might, now stands cheek-by-jowl with tidily inoffensive houses.

Despite the lack of inspiration in much of Liverpool's post-war rebuilding, recent years have seen a return of confidence, a renaissance buoyed by the 2004 listing of the heart of the city and its docks as a World Heritage Site and the accolade of European Capital of Culture in 2008. Some of the best new work has been in the regeneration of redundant historic buildings, ranging from adaptation of the 1930s Speke Airport terminal building into a hotel and the former Midland Railway 1874 goods warehouse in Whitechapel into the museum's conservation centre to well-executed warehouse conversions in the Duke Street area and the creation of apartments in Elmes's 1843 Collegiate Institution, on Shaw Street. Liverpool-trained architects feature prominently. The work of Jim Eyre of Wilkinson Eyre, Rod McAllister of King McAllister and Jonathan Falkingham of Urban Splash perpetuate a century-old tradition of Liverpool architects leaving a mark on their city.

Today, despite losses sustained during the Blitz and the 'redevelopment years' that started in the 1950s, Liverpool still possesses more listed buildings (1,471 entries relating to 2,500 individual buildings) than any city outside London.

The former Liverpool Collegiate on Shaw Street. *Neil Cossons*

THE EXCHANGE

LEFT: The epicentre of Liverpool's commercial activity was the first Exchange, built in 1808 on the site of the town's early markets. In 1862, this four-storey building in the French Renaissance style was opened with more storeys and more commodious office space, plus a fine news room in its west wing. *Clive Garner collection*

LEFT: In the late 1930s it was replaced by the present Exchange building, completed in 1955. The open quadrangle area ('The Flags') was a major meeting place for traders and brokers with shops and vaults underneath, later converted into a car park. The centrepiece of The Flags is the Nelson memorial (1813). Designed by Mathew Wyatt, it is the city's first public monument. In the vicinity of the Exchange, the Town Hall and other nearby major commercial buildings were several dining rooms where cohorts of office workers would have their lunch, many businessmen regularly indulging in long, three-course lunches with suitable liquid refreshment! *John Collingwood collection*

CUSTOM HOUSE

One of the major casualties of World War 2 was the Custom House, one of several notable public buildings designed by John Foster Junior (1787-1846), who from 1801 was the Town Surveyor. Erected between 1828-39, it occupied the site of New Dock and was originally designed to act as excise office, post office and dock office. Escalating costs led to some of the more flamboyant architectural features being dropped from the design, but this aerial view illustrates clearly how it dominated Canning Place and the older commercial areas of the port. The northern portico faced towards Derby Square while the west side looked towards the docks and river. Also in view are the half-completed Anglican Cathedral and the tall steeple of St Michael's Church (late 1820s), modelled on St Martin-in-the-Fields in London. After sustaining major war damage, the Custom House's shell was eventually knocked down, the site occupied during the 1960s by Steers House, a nondescript office complex demolished in 2000. During recent archaeological excavations, parts of New Dock (built 1715) were uncovered and carefully recorded; some sections are displayed within the new shopping development, Liverpool One. *Clive Garner collection*

135-139 DALE STREET c1788

This noble trio of brick townhouses are the last remnants of 18th-century Dale Street before it was widened. No 139 was built for John Houghton, a distiller, whose works were nearby; with its front elevation onto Trueman Street, it is both the best and the least altered.
J. G. Parkinson,
Online Transport Archive

FORMER BANK OF ENGLAND, CASTLE STREET

The Bank of England built three branches outside London – in Manchester, Liverpool and Bristol – all designed by C. R. Cockerell (1788-1863), of which Liverpool's is the largest and grandest. Its presence not only confirms Castle Street's importance as the axis of the commercial quarter, but emphasises the wider role of the city as a global mercantile and financial centre. Completed in 1848, this is one of Cockerell's greatest works, a tour de force of bravura Victorian commercial architecture. It demonstrates brilliantly how the monumental use of classical orders – in this case Greek and Roman Doric – can signify power and authority. At the front of the building was residential accommodation for the bank's Liverpool agent, with the subagent's house at the other, entered off Cook Street.
Neil Cossons

ALBANY BUILDINGS, OLD HALL STREET

Completed in 1858 to the design by J. K. Colling, in the style of an Italian palazzo, as a combined office and warehouse Albany Buildings was much used by cotton brokers. The spacious courtyard crossed by two iron footbridges, each with a spiral staircase, provided their meeting place. Natural light from top-lit glazed corridors ensured good conditions for the examination of cotton samples. There were iron cranes on the side elevations serving basement storage areas and magnificent gates cast locally by Rankin's Union Foundry to look like wrought-iron. These led to the vaulted corridor, giving access to the courtyard. The building is now an apartment block.
Neil Cossons

LIVERPOOL & LONDON INSURANCE BUILDING, DALE STREET, 1855-58

This great Venetian palazzo-style complex occupies the important corner site next to the Town Hall. Another Cockerell design, it is one of the city's grandest and most distinguished buildings. The front block, with its powerful entrance of polished red granite festooned above with heavy garlands, was built for the insurance company; the three blocks at the back were for letting. The original atrium that provided light to the offices that surrounded it has been built over. Today it is occupied by the Royal Bank of Scotland. *Neil Cossons*

ORIEL CHAMBERS

Built in 1864, this is one of the city's architectural treasures. The most innovative and influential of buildings, it was far ahead of its time and a precursor by 20 years of the frame- and curtain-wall buildings of Chicago and New York. Built to the designs of Liverpool architect Peter Ellis (1808-88), it stands on the corner of Water Street and Covent Garden. The building has an iron frame, built of standardised prefabricated units, from which are cantilevered projecting oriel windows, each with the most slender of iron glazing bars, flooding the interiors with natural light. The windows, in standing proud from the frame, give the appearance of a continuously glazed exterior. In fact, the verticals between the windows are clad in stone and project upwards to a stone parapet. The courtyard, accessible through the passage off Water Street to the left of the entrance, reveals in its much simpler style an even more breathtaking elevation with the glazing cantilevered out from the frame. The north end of the building, fronting onto Covent Garden, was badly damaged in the Blitz and rebuilt (1959-61) to harmonise with the original.

Strongly disparaged in professional journals at the time of its construction, Oriel Chambers was a prophetic forerunner of 20th-century city architecture. The young American architect John Wellborn Root (1850-81), who studied in Liverpool as a young man before returning to work with Daniel H. Burnham, a fellow founder of the Chicago school of architecture, is thought to have been much influenced by Oriel Chambers. *Neil Cossons*

16 COOK STREET

This is Ellis's only other known building (built 1866). Also startlingly modern in appearance and iron-framed, it possesses an extraordinary ratio of glass to frame. Five storeys high, it has narrow vertical ribs of stone, rising to an arched top. At the rear, the offices facing the courtyard also have huge glazed areas with a cantilevered spiral staircase. Ellis lived for a time at 40 Falkner Square, now marked by an English Heritage blue plaque. *Neil Cossons*

COMPTON HOUSE

This heavily-ornate, mid-Victorian building of 1867, with its fireproof interior, still stands on the east side of Church Street. Reflecting Liverpool's commercial pre-eminence, Compton House was one of the first purpose-built department stores in the world. Designed by Thomas Haig & Sons for J. R. Jeffrey, it had replaced an earlier store destroyed by fire. In 1895, the French Renaissance-style four-storey building still had its high pavilion roofs (since removed) and the upper floors housed workshops and staff accommodation. The imposing entrance with a figure of Commerce above is flanked on both sides by bays, while the entrance from the corner with Tarleton Street provided access to the Compton Hotel (closed 1929). To the left, the Italian-style building was designed in the 1850s by Thomas Hornblower for Elkington's, who dealt in cutlery, metal work and electroplating. Today it is occupied by Clarks, while Compton House is home to Marks & Spencer. *F. Frith, Martin Jenkins, David Packer and Jerome McWatt, Online Transport Archive*

All three waterfront buildings, the Royal Liver Building (left), the Cunard Building (centre) and the MD&HB Building (right) are seen in September 1954.
J. B. C. McCann, Online Transport Archive

THE WATERFRONT

The most visible symbol of Liverpool's commercial might is the group of three great buildings at George's Pier Head. Built on in-filled George's Dock, they have become the city's signature, creating one of the most famous skylines in the world and the focal point of the World Heritage Site.

First to be built was the MD&HB Building – now the Port of Liverpool Building – the result of a competition won by architects Briggs and Wolstenhome. This monumental rectangular structure is built around a steel frame encased in concrete and faced in Portland stone in an exuberantly baroque style, with polygonal corner turrets and stone cupolas. The figures of Commerce and Industry flank the entrance leading through to a full-height octagonal hall beneath the central dome. Around its base is inscribed: 'They that go down to the sea in ships that do business in great waters these see the works of the Lord and his wonders of the deep. Anno Domini MCMVII.' It is difficult to express more clearly the

meaning and purpose of this building. Anchor chain, anchors, dolphins, mermaids, tridents and seahorses abound. In the stained glass windows are dedications to the dominions and colonies of the British Empire. This is mercantile might and imperial power writ large.

The second building is the Grade 1 listed Royal Liver Building (left, built 1911), the home of the Royal Liver Friendly Society, set up in the city in 1850. This is the first major British building – and one of the first in the world – to be built of reinforced concrete. It was poured *in situ* and then the building was clad in granite. Designed by Walter Aubrey Thomas, at 295 feet it was the city's tallest building until completion of St John's Beacon in 1965. It shows signs of American influence in its detailing, crowned by a pair of towers with clock faces 25 feet in diameter, larger than those of Big Ben. Atop each stand the mythical Liver Birds, designed by Carl Bernard Bartels and cast in copper – once gilded – on a steel frame. The building remains the head office for the Royal Liver

Friendly Society and is alleged to be the Gothic inspiration for both the Manhattan Municipal Building in New York and the Seven Sisters in Moscow.

In the gap between these two waterfront monsters is the Cunard Building, completed in 1916 as the headquarters of the Cunard Steamship Company. An Italian Renaissance palazzo on a gigantic scale, it was designed by William Willink and Philip Thicknesse, although recent research indicates more plural parentage. The building served both as offices and terminal, with facilities including separate waiting rooms for first-, second- and third-class passengers, a booking hall, luggage storage space and currency exchange. Cunard merged with White Star in 1934 to become the world's largest passenger liner carrier, with headquarters in this building. In the 1960s, Cunard relocated its UK operations to Southampton and its global headquarters to New York. It subsequently sold the Cunard Building to Prudential plc in 1969, who, in 2001, sold it again, to the Merseyside Pension Fund.

RIGHT: When the Liver Building was cleaned and refurbished, decades of soot and grime were removed. *Neil Cossons*

ALBION HOUSE
(FORMER WHITE STAR BUILDING)

ABOVE: This prominent building at the corner of James Street and The Strand was designed by Norman Shaw (1831-1912) as the headquarters of the White Star Line, and completed in 1898. Drawing inspiration from the nearby tall warehouses, this was the first of the new breed of giant office buildings and still more than holds its own today. The lower section is in the form of a massive granite plinth, above which is a memorable mix of Portland stone, red brick and domed corner turrets, all derived directly from Shaw's earlier New Scotland Yard (built 1890). The interior is remarkable for the prominence of the exposed iron girders – the rivets and bolts highlighted for effect – and brick jack-arches. At this building, which housed all facilities for first-, second- and third-class White Star passengers, staff learned of the loss of the *Titanic* in 1912. After the 1934 merger with Cunard, the building passed to the Pacific Steam Navigation Company. By the time the PSNCo ceased to exist, in 1985, the British Merchant fleet consisted of 920 ships, or three per cent of world tonnage, compared with 48 per cent in 1900.

Albion House has enjoyed something of a charmed life. Damaged by fire in 1923 and again during bombing in 1941, it survived, although some architectural features had to be removed. There is a large mosaic map of South America on the floor of the entrance hall, a part of its PSNCo history. *A. S. Clayton, Online Transport Archive*

FORMER BRITISH & FOREIGN MARINE INSURANCE COMPANY BUILDING, 1890

Designed by Grayson & Ould, this building exemplifies the increasing popularity of brick and terracotta. The mosaic frieze with shipping scenes was designed by Frank Murray and made by Antonio Salviati (1816-90) of Venice. *Neil Cossons*

INDIA BUILDINGS, WATER STREET, 1924-31

This is one of the city's largest office buildings, a nine-storey steel-framed structure occupying a whole block on the south side of Water Street. Built for Alfred Holt's Blue Funnel Line to the5designs of Herbert J. Rowse (it was the winning of this commission that launched his career) India Buildings exemplifies the refined classical style typical of North American 1920s office blocksof which Rowse was an enthusiastic proponent. Such is its5immense size, it was supposedly designed so it could be converted into a warehouse if the offices failed to let. Another American feature is a barrel-vaulted arcade, lined with shops, which runs through its centre. Badly damaged during the Blitz, it was rebuilt under Rowse's supervision. *Martin Jenkins collection, Online Transport Archive*

FORMER MARTINS BANK, WATER STREET, 1927-32

BELOW: A key element for business people was a reliable and regular postal service. This example of one of the unique 1863 'Liverpool Special' cast-iron hexagonal letterboxes, with their distinctive crowns, was photographed on Edge Lane in 1969. *Neil Cossons*

ABOVE: Opposite India Buildings and dominating the north side of Water Street stands another Rowse masterpiece, the equally monumental, American-style former headquarters of Martins Bank, now Barclays. The winner of a competition judged by Charles Reilly, Rowse's former Professor at the School of Architecture, its use of Portland stone on a steel frame is another example of North American 'office classicism', for which Rowse and Reilly were enthusiasts. This is one of the best interwar buildings in Britain and symbolises the contemporary stature of Martins, the only major bank to have head offices outside London.

In 1940, Britain's gold reserves were placed in the vaults en route to Canada. Martins was taken over by the Bank of Liverpool (founded in 1831) in 1918, the amalgamated banks changing their combined name to Martins in 1928. When acquired by Barclays in 1969, it had 700 branches. *Clive Garner collection*

Until the Municipal Reform Act of 1835 a small coterie of privileged freemen, who had purchased rather than earned their positions, exploited the twin forces of Protestantism and protectionism to control Liverpool and ensure its working-class Protestant base opposed 'unpatriotic' free trade promoted by the Liberals. To enhance their wealth, these men willingly financed rebuilding some parts of the town and encouraged the development of the Dock Estate, but they also drove shipbuilding from the waterfront and opposed the coming of the railway. Under them, Liverpool was known as 'the biggest rotten borough in England'. Their determination to restrict public spending effectively increased social problems, which subsequent town councils struggled to overcome.

Since its inception in 1797, the Town Hall has witnessed numerous turbulent periods. For over 100 years, from 1842-1955, Liverpool was ruled by a Tory Protestant establishment. Although a Labour councillor was elected in 1902, it was only after the 1911 transport strike that a Labour group was elected. The Conservative defeat of 1955 virtually ended sectarian politics, although a Protestant Party candidate did seek election as late as 1973.

After a period of volatility with hung councils, tensions increased during the mid-1980s, when power was vested in the local Labour group dominated by the Militant Tendency and their radical agenda. More recently, Labour and the Liberal Democrats have both held power, each striving to be more accountable, democratic and inclusive.

Local politics has never followed a normal path in Liverpool. For years it was far from democratic and blighted by 'irregularities'. Some legendary political figures wielded power and patronage akin to American city bosses, including Edward Whitley, A. B. Forwood, Austin Harford, Archibald Salvidge, John Braddock and Derek Hatton.

In 2008, Liverpool was named by the Audit Commission as having the worst financially managed council in England, despite having over 30 officials earning in excess of £100,000 per annum.

Marcus Eavis, Online Transport Archive

TOWN HALL

Liverpool Town Hall is the city's most magnificent Georgian building and has some of the finest civic interiors in the country. Its banqueting hall, ballroom, grand staircase and reception rooms have, in recent years, been splendidly restored and are in regular public use. Standing at the north end of Castle Street, at the junction with Dale Street and Water Street, the building was originally designed as The Exchange by John Wood the Elder of Bath (1704-54) for commercial and municipal purposes, with the work supervised by his son John, (1728-82). It opened in 1754 but, following a disastrous fire in 1795, most of the interior was destroyed. It was then rebuilt and reopened as the Town Hall in 1797, to the designs of James Wyatt (1746-1813). Subsequent additions include the dome and cupola (1802) and the extended portico (1811), both the work of Wyatt, and the council chamber (1900).

Over the years the building has been a symbolic focal point at times of local and national celebration. In the first view it is dressed overall for the Coronation of Edward VII and in the second, it proudly celebrates the City's 800th anniversary in 2007.

Glynn Parry collection and Neil Cossons

MUNICIPAL BUILDING

One of the original seven thoroughfares, Dale Street has undergone many changes. Once narrow and straggling, and surrounded by some of the city's poorest housing, breweries, factories, coaching inns and taverns, it was transformed during the second half of the 19th century. To create the space for the Municipal Building, older buildings – including three coaching inns, *The Old White Lion*, *The Saracen's Head* and *The Flying Horse* – were demolished in the 1850s, the site occupied from 1857-61 by *Hengler's Circus*. After enjoying considerable success, Hengler later returned to Liverpool to build the Hippodrome on West Derby Road.

The Corporation needed a new building to accommodate its expanding staff. Completed in 1868 to the designs of John Weightman, modified by E. R. Robson, the Municipal Building's great central atrium and huge pyramidal tower, in the manner of Charles Barry's Halifax Town Hall, make it a vivid symbol of Liverpool's newfound civic grandeur. Other nearby public buildings eventually included the Main Bridewell prison, the magistrates' courts, tramways offices and fire station. Also visible on the south side in this 1886 photograph are the French Renaissance-style Conservative Club building (built 1883), Imperial Chambers (1870s) and the red sandstone Musker's Building (1881-82). Water carts 5 and 60 are either conveying fresh water or spraying the streets to lay the dust, while tram 181 is plodding east away from the Pier Head.

F. Frith, Martin Jenkins, David Packer and Jerome Watt, Online Transport Archive

THE CULTURAL CITY

ST GEORGE'S HALL

St George's Hall ranks among the finest neo-classical buildings in Europe. It was designed by a young architectural prodigy, Harvey Lonsdale Elmes (1813-47), who won a design competition to satisfy Liverpool's long-felt need for a hall for musical events and other large gatherings. At the same time, the city sought a design for new assize courts on an adjacent site. Elmes won this competition too and soon there were moves to combine both projects. Elmes' third design, although much modified during construction, resulted in the present building, as near as Liverpool gets to its Coliseum.

Imperial pretensions are evident throughout. The site, the building's gigantic scale – and especially the great south front towering over St John's Lane – all enabled Liverpool to emphasise its civilised and civic values as the counterpoint to commerce. Nevertheless, the concert hall triumphantly celebrates Liverpool and its port, with the city coat of arms and numerous sea nymphs, dolphins and tridents. It is one of Britain's greatest Victorian interiors. Externally, the huge bronze doors, with no pretension of modesty, adapt the SPQR motto of Rome: 'the Senate and People of Liverpool'; entwined dolphins

In this 1895 scene, the sculpted pediment (the sculptures themselves were removed in the 1950s as unsafe) was still in existence on the south portico. Over the years, the expansive plateau has been the venue for many public gatherings. To the left is the mid-18th century St John's Church, which was demolished in 1899 and the churchyard transformed into St John's Gardens (1904). It was the close proximity of St John's which, it is claimed, led to the simplified design of the west face of St George's Hall, apparent today. *F. Frith, Martin Jenkins, David Packer and Jerome McWatt, Online Transport Archive.*

support the lamp standards. Elmes died in 1847 and C. R. Cockerell, then in his late fifties, assembled the brilliant remnants he had left and shaped them into a glorious whole. The building was noted too for its revolutionary form of circulation heating and ventilation.

Two sculptures of local worthies are of particular interest to this book: George Stephenson (1781-1848) and Henry Booth (1789-1869), engineer and promoter of the Liverpool & Manchester Railway. Stephenson (completed 1851) appears in classical garb as the sculptor felt he should 'look like Archimedes', while Booth, added in 1874, has his left hand resting on the screw-coupling of his own invention. Beneath is a scroll with a drawing of Stephenson's *Rocket*, designed with Booth's involvement. The screw-coupling, patented by Booth in 1836, was a boon in improving comfort and safety on passenger trains.

All four sides of the building are different and some alterations have been made over the years. Following war damage, extensive repairs were undertaken. With the departure of the law courts to new buildings in the 1980s, there was even talk of demolition, but common sense prevailed and a major programme of renovation, including full refurbishment of the organ, meant that the concert hall played a major role during Liverpool's European Capital of Culture celebrations in 2008.

With the building of St George's Hall, the opportunity arose to create a great civic forum 'round which could be clustered our handsomest edifices'. In the event, the development of what had been the ramshackle area of Shaw's Brow was rather piecemeal, with an uneven line of buildings along what is now William Brown Street. But the result was spectacular. Local pride and philanthropy combined to provide the city with cultural institutions and a county court which, as an ensemble, are without equal.

MUSEUM AND LIBRARY

The free public library and museum (built 1860) was designed by Corporation surveyor John Weightman, and financed by the prominent merchant and banker William Brown MP (1784-1864), in whose honour the street was renamed. The long, rather severe neo-classical façade was designed to flank an open plateau complementing St George's Hall, from which the building takes its cues. This view dates from the end of the 19th century. The present steps up to the original museum entrance are a later addition, inserted when the plateau was removed for construction of the museum extension and Central Technical School (1901). Following severe bomb damage in 1941, the museum was rebuilt behind the original façade. The interior of the library was rebuilt between 1957-60 (subsequently extended in 1978) and the museum between 1963-9. *Liverpool Public Record Office*

PICTON READING ROOM

ABOVE: Further up from the museum is the Picton Reading Room (opened 1879). Named after the chairman of the council's Museum and Arts Committee, James Picton, it has a domed roof and attractive, colonnaded, semi-circular façade which neatly forms the hinge for the change in direction of the William Brown Street frontage. Drawing inspiration from the British Museum Reading Room, architect Cornelius Sherlock designed a similar high, circular space surrounded by stacks and galleries. *Liverpool Public Record Office*

RIGHT: Cultural aspirations blossomed under the Victorians. Some 25 branch libraries were eventually built, including several provided by the Carnegie Foundation. Great emphasis was placed on books for children. The libraries were built in contrasting styles, and this fascinating example is the Everton branch on St Domingo Road, now closed. *Neil Cossons*

WALKER ART GALLERY AND THE TECHNICAL COLLEGE

Also on William Brown Street is the Walker Art Gallery (built 1877), designed by architects Cornelius Sherlock and H. H. Vale and financed by the brewer (and Mayor of Liverpool) Andrew Barclay Walker. Its entrance, which observes the neo-classical niceties of the area, is watched over by the seated figures of Raphael and Michelangelo. Originally intended to display contemporary art, the gallery soon assembled a fine permanent collection, one of the best outside London. It doubled in size between 1882-4, and in the early 1930s an extension, designed by Andrew Thornely, was built at the rear. Recently, the gap between the original building and the 1930s extension has been partially filled by a new first-floor foyer. In 1986, both the museum and the Walker gallery were transferred from what was then Merseyside County Council to a government-funded board of trustees – National Museums Liverpool – a rare and possibly unique example of nationalisation by the Thatcher administration, justified on the one hand by the outstanding quality of the collections and on the other by the desire to keep the museum and gallery out of the hands of the then dysfunctional city council. *Liverpool Public Record Office*

ABOVE: The Technical College (1901) was to the designs of E. W. Mountford. The lower floor, with access from Byrom Street, originally housed the Technical College whilst the upper levels provided additional gallery space for the Museum. Now the building is given over entirely to the Museum. In this view taken in 1968, Byrom Street is in the process of redevelopment. *J. G. Parkinson, Online Transport Archive*

VICTORIA BUILDING

RIGHT: Liverpool University was granted its charter in 1903. Prior to that, the fledgling University College (1881) was, with Manchester, part of the Victoria University. The main seat of learning was established on Brownlow Hill. Dominating this 1965 vista, photographed looking east from the Walker Engineering Laboratories, is the redbrick and terracotta Victoria Building (1892) with its Jubilee Tower, designed by the Liverpool-born architect Alfred Waterhouse (1830-1905). It served initially as the principal administrative and teaching building and has a glorious double-height entrance hall, rich in Burmantofts glazed tiles. The clock was the gift of W. F. Hartley, the jam magnate.

In 1943, writing under the pseudonym Bruce Truscot, Edgar Allison Peers (1891-1952), the university's Gilmour Professor of Spanish, published a book on the new alternatives to the ancient seats of learning, about an institution founded in the provinces during the Victorian years and unencumbered by the weight of tradition. The title of his book, *Redbrick University*, originated the now familiar term. Not until after Peers' death in 1952 was he finally identified as the author, and 'redbrick' became irrevocably associated in Liverpool and further afield with the blood-red luminescence of the Victoria Building. The building has recently been restored internally and externally, and reopened in 2008 as the Victoria Gallery & Museum for the display of the university's collections. Demolition to the east has totally obliterated steeply-graded Paddington. *B. D. Pyne, Online Transport Archive*

RIGHT: Standing diagonally across from the Victoria Building is the Guild of Students (1913). Designed by Charles Reilly in a 'Liverpool classical' style, it is regarded as one of his major works. What was originally the 'women's side' has a grand domestic frontage with a first-floor bow window; the 'men's side' is in contrasting style to emphasise the division. The largely windowless north face originally overlooked the railway cutting to Lime Street Station; when this was decked over and the building cleaned for the first time, 'the Guild' came into its own. *Neil Cossons*

URBAN DEVELOPMENT VIII

TOWARDS A HEALTHY AND WHOLESOME CITY

The Victorians recognised the importance of parks and recreation grounds as 'green lungs', which allowed people to escape from inner-city pollution and indulge in healthy exercise. Financed by a wealthy iron merchant and designed by James Paxton and James Pennethorne, Prince's Park opened initially as a private park *c* 1842, fringed by quality housing. Impressed by the concept, the Corporation envisaged a ring of parks each flanked by similar housing, the rents from which would help towards the upkeep. The largest and most memorable of these is Sefton Park (269 acres).

Generations of Liverpudlians have enjoyed the city's parks, with their band concerts, boating lakes, bowling greens, children's playgrounds, cricket and football pitches, floral displays, golf courses, open-air drama and opera productions, picnic sites, Punch and Judy shows, tennis courts and skating. Some public spaces, like St Domingo's Pit in Everton, served as venues for volatile sectarian meetings and, in 1912, 12 processions totalling 100,000 people opposed to Irish Home Rule converged on Newsham & Sheil Park. When it opened in 1950, Otterspool promenade gave access to the waterfront after many years. Today, long stretches are once again accessible to the public.

Liverpool's apparently unstoppable economic momentum was its most important characteristic during the 18th century, reflected in the increasingly graceful style of its fine buildings and the improvements designed to aid commerce. Through a succession of Improvement Acts, Liverpool's renewal plans far outstripped those of other cities in their scale and ambition. Between 1771 and 1832, £645,891 was spent on widening streets and improving routes in and out of town, much of it on buying buildings – often owned by members of the town

Sefton Park (1872) provides a fine example of a well-planned municipal park. Designed by the French horticulturalist Édouard André (1840-1911) and Liverpool architect Lewis Hornblower (1823-78), it is one of the most important of the great Victorian urban parks in Britain. Today, visitors can admire the surrounding houses, the gates and lodges, the landscaped parkland, lake, obelisk and the statue of William Rathbone, one of the major Unitarian philanthropists. But the pièce de résistance is the stunning octagonal Palm House (1896). Designed and built by the Edinburgh company of Mackenzie and Moncur Ltd, it makes full use of cast iron components and was fully restored in 2001. *Neil Cossons*

Of the 90,000 destitute rural Irish who fled to Liverpool during the first three months of 1847, a fifth died from malnutrition and fever. While some migrated to America, many were simply absorbed into the already overcrowded slums plagued by outbreaks of cholera, dysentery, typhus, smallpox and other infectious diseases. The town authorities tended to look the other way, relying on charities and philanthropists to finance relief. However, they did accept the need for a permanent supply of pure drinking water. Prior to the Liverpool Sanitary Act of 1846 and the appointment of Thomas Duncan as the first Water Engineer, piped water sold from carts often cost more than beer or spirits. To supplement supplies from local wells, reservoirs were opened in the Rivington Watershed (1857, 23 miles) and at Lake Vyrnwy (1891, 60 miles), from where water was pumped to local service reservoirs built on high ground such as the one in Everton seen above. It was designed by Duncan with a bowling green and recreation ground on its upper level. Although still working and upgraded in 1980, the original reservoirs are filled in. Owing to the narrow roads in this vicinity, inbound and outbound trams used different streets until 1956. The tram seen here was inbound on Aubrey Street. *H. B. Priestley, National Tramway Museum*

council – for demolition. With a strong and cohesive civic authority, on a socially and geographically manageable scale, the council was able to have a significant influence on the way in which the town grew, via regulating the leases of wealthy merchants – at least in the nature and scope of its newer and better-off areas.

Evidence of this can still be seen today. As ground landlord of much of the town then available to developers, it was able to exercise control over the layout of new streets, to prevent the incursion of industrial businesses into residential areas, to ensure standards for elevations of new buildings and to ban cellar dwellings. Fashionable squares were laid out, comparable with those in London, and terraces of distinguished town houses reflected thoughtful estate management on the part of the city fathers, as well as the self-interest of the oligarchy that formed their membership.

In a determined drive to alleviate the lot of the poor, and to overcome endemic disease by providing good quality accommodation at affordable rents (for some), the Corporation built the first municipally-owned housing in Britain in 1869. Designed to a high standard, ranging from one to four rooms, it set a pattern for the future. The city's reputation as a provider grew during the rest of the century; even after national legislation in 1919 required local authorities to provide social housing, Liverpool continued to lead the way. By then the Corporation owned and managed 2,895 dwellings, more than ten per cent of the country's total of council houses. Ten years later that number had grown to nearly 22,000. However, the problem throughout for the council and its officials was to keep pace with demand and, in particular, to provide housing within the reach of the poorest. Sometimes new housing, often outside the immediate central areas, was simply beyond the means of the very poorest, and as late as 1934, 'the inconvenience and cost to the casual and low-paid dock labourer of living at any great distance from his work [were] among the major factors of the Merseyside housing problem.' In 1946, weekly rents varied according to the number of rooms, the cheapest costing approximately six shillings (30p) and the most expensive 11 shillings (65p).

During the later part of the 19th century, Liverpool became a leading player in civic design as the city formulated radical yet strategic solutions to secure its future. In 1908, the University of Liverpool established the world's first department for the study of town

Duncan's monumental, 90-foot, sandstone Water Tower (built 1857) is on Margaret Street. Today, the third tier of the original pump house has gone; the second pump house was added in the 1860s. The cast-iron circular tank rests on the stone arches of the former pumping house. The Industrial Revolution transformed Everton from a leafy village into an area of mass housing, much of which was cleared during the 1960s and 1970s. This is one of the most conspicuous mid-Victorian public buildings to survive. *Nigel Bowker*

LEFT: As a result of the 1846 Sanitary Act, several key officials were appointed. James Newlands was responsible for cleansing, sewerage and road improvements and Dr William Henry Duncan, appalled by Liverpool's reputation as 'the black spot on the Mersey', railroaded the Council into making him the world's first Medical Officer of Health, after which he fought to improve overall conditions by building public baths and washhouses. *John Collingwood collection*

LEFT BOTTOM: The women seen walking to a washhouse in 1952 owed much to Kitty Wilkinson who, having identified unwashed clothes as a prime carrier of disease, spent hours boiling her cholera-stricken neighbours' clothing. It was her determination to defeat 'Dr Death' which resulted in the first washhouse in 1842. Buried in St James Cemetery, her achievements are commemorated by a memorial window in the cathedral. The last reported cholera epidemic was in 1866. *Liverpool Public Record Office*

planning. Its graduates were among the first to pioneer urban planning as an essential requirement for the considered and strategic growth of cities. The Corporation's innovations also received worldwide acclaim, especially after the appointment in 1925 of Sir Lancelot Keay (1883-1974) as City Architect and Director of Housing. During his tenure, the city built over 35,000 houses and flats and he was also responsible for the creation of the pre-war township of Speke, an international model for self-contained municipal housing estates.

RIGHT: Rodney Street epitomises the city's Georgian quarter. This long, elegantly terraced street was laid out in 1783-4. However, despite its impressiveness as a wide, straight, desirable residential thoroughfare, it was developed piecemeal over some 30 years within general conditions set by the Corporation. Those who could afford it enjoyed an elevated location away from the congested lower part of the town. Generally consisting of three- or five-bay houses built in brick, individually or in short runs, it has an overall appearance of uniformity. Once 'Liverpool's Harley Street', today it has the more pluralistic but still generally prosperous feel of being at the heart of an area coming up in the world, but with very few single dwelling residences. *Neil Cossons*

LEFT: This fine row of brick three-storey houses (built c1810) on Seymour Street was developed by John Foster Junior, who may also have been the architect. Refurbishment as offices in the early 1990s, by Inner City Enterprises, involved preservation of the façades and rebuilding of the interiors. *Neil Cossons*

TOP: Canning Street (built in the 1820s) is one of the best preserved of the once considerable number of long, residential 19th-century streets in Georgian Liverpool; its owners, the City Council and English Heritage, have reversed decades of decay. Laid out to provide a link with the town centre, it consists of mainly brick-built three-bay terraces, with three storeys above a semi-basement. *Neil Cossons*

MIDDLE: The first six houses on Gambier Terrace were built in the early 1830s, by the developer Ambrose Lace. One of the most impressive terraces in the city, its magnificent composition is enhanced by its dramatic location overlooking the great pit of St James's cemetery. After a long spell in the doldrums, the fortunes of this fine piece of speculative housing, completed in the 1870s, are reviving in response to investment in the surrounding streets and the renewed confidence that has spread from it. *Cedric Greenwood*

BOTTOM: Contrasting with Rodney Street and Gambier Terrace were the infamous court dwellings (built in the 1780s), another consciously-developed architectural form, but intended in this instance to cram as many as possible into the smallest possible space. Mass immigration, a large casual labour force and very low wage levels all led to the building of high-density accommodation, including courts in the areas close to the docks and central area, over which the town council had no control.

Relying on casual labour in the docks, men needed to be within walking distance of potential places of employment and so, for decades, Liverpool had some of the shortest journey-to-work distances of any British city. Those with regular and usually better paid work lived outside of the area and could afford public transport. These divisions were reflected in the housing, which led to a sharp segregation of people and the type of buildings which they occupied.

In 1801, about 15 per cent of the population lived in courts which had only basic water and sanitation, lacked light and fresh air and suffered high rates of infant mortality. By 1895 there were over 1,500 courts, with the final handful surviving until the 1960s. In 1850, Liverpool journalist Hugh Shimmin provided this vivid description: 'These court houses are frequently four storeys high, "straight up and down", and contain four apartments – a cellar, a living room, and two bedrooms; and often in these houses two and sometimes three families reside. The houses adjoining these are sometimes let at a lower rent: thus poor creatures have a premium offered them for the loss of their health and the possibility of cutting short their days.'
Liverpool Public Record Office

RIGHT: An alternative to the courts were the thousands of damp, poorly-lit cellars which, by 1801, housed some 12 per cent of the population. Moves to eradicate these repugnant dwellings began as early as the 1840s, although 27,000 people lived in 11,000 cellars in 1849. Although condemned as 'unfit for human habitation', even as late as 1912 some 5,000 people lived in 1,600 cellars, these being mainly the families of poor marine firemen, carters, charwomen and casual dock labourers. *Liverpool Public Record Office*

RIGHT: 'There is probably no city of anything like equal size in which so small a proportion of the population is maintained by permanent and stable work. The principal occupation of the city and the foundation of its prosperity is the handling of goods between ship, warehouse and railway; a function which is mainly performed by unskilled labour.' Casual labour, the type of occupation – if any – and drunkenness often defined the areas of lowest quality housing. Salt-heaving, fruit hawking, cotton and oakum picking and road sweeping were among casual occupations that men no longer strong enough to work on the docks might find. For women too, casual work was often all that was available. Many unfortunate people relied increasingly on Poor Law relief or assistance from numerous charities which had been active since the early 18th century, most notably in the setting up of the Bluecoat School in 1709 for the education of poor and orphaned children. By the 19th century there were many more, often with overlapping interests, resulting in the three main charities coming together in 1863 as the Central Relief Society. Influential local families, especially the Rathbones, were powerful supporters of these charities, as were the churches. *Neil Cossons*

ABOVE LEFT: An entrance into St Martin's Cottages (built 1869), the oldest municipal housing in Britain. When the estate opened there were six well-designed blocks, consisting of 124 tenements each with a scullery and separate toilet. Most importantly, washing boilers were also provided. *A. S. Clayton, Online Transport Archive*

ABOVE: Plenty of space for washing, gossiping and keeping an eye on things. *J. E. Marsh*

ABOVE: Sir Thomas White Gardens, off St Domingo Road, was once the site of many long-vanished, Corporation-built, high-density flats. Encompassing an open courtyard, the landing flats on the five storeys were accessed from a central stairwell. By October 1967, there would have been hot and cold running water, internal plumbing and a resident caretaker.

RIGHT: The time-honoured tradition of scrubbing the step, this one leading into a long-vanished doctor's surgery in the north end. *Both A. S. Clayton, Online Transport Archive*

ABOVE: These rare examples of early 20th-century, cottage-style council houses, with their half-timbered gables, still exist on Eldon Grove. When they were built, they contrasted with other more austere designs and, later, with bleak blocks such as the infamous 1960s 'Piggeries'. Converted for use as student accommodation, by 2010 they were in a state of disrepair.

BELOW: Most large blocks had a play area for children, while there were also designated 'play streets' with displayed restrictions on vehicle movements. *Both A. S. Clayton, Online Transport Archive*

RIGHT: A back-entry 'jigger' in Everton. *Neil Cossons*

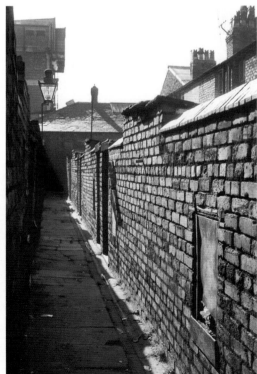

TOP: Between the wars, the Corporation built over half the city's new housing stock and its high-quality suburban estates, served by trams on segregated reserved tracks (foreground), had a major impact on the geography of the city and its appearance. Even today, after 30 years of right-to-buy legislation, they remain impressive for the careful integration of their design. While 'the Corpy' catered for the most needy, it was assumed that housing for the better off would be met by the private sector.
A. S. Clayton,
Online Transport Archive

MIDDLE: Built in the 1920s and named after the contractor, the 2,000-house Boot Estate, in Norris Green, had brick-built houses around its edge while those in the centre were made of prefabricated concrete sections using power-station clinker residue. Classed as 'defective dwellings' under the 1985 Housing Act, demolition has been slow; empty houses have been targeted by vandals, booby-trapped or set on fire.
Neil Cossons

BOTTOM: In the years before World War 2, Lancelot Keay had a profound effect on the city's suburban landscape with his distinctive neo-Georgian style of council housing. Built in large numbers from a palette of standard designs, they permeate many areas of the city inside and outside the ring of Queens Drive, these examples being on East Prescot Road, Knotty Ash. Under the Housing Act 1980, tenants were given the right to buy their council houses, resulting in a pandemonium of self-expression breaking up the carefully choreographed symmetry of Keay's designs.
Neil Cossons

RIGHT: Liverpool-trained architect John Hughes (1903-1977) was taken onto Keay's staff in 1931. His design for St Andrews Gardens (1934-5) was inspired by the Horseshoe Estate in Berlin, with its smooth vertical exterior and continuous balconies overlooking a central court. Restored and provided with lifts in the 1990s as student accommodation, it is the best of the few remaining, large, brick-built 1930s blocks of walk-up flats. Hughes went on from Liverpool to Manchester and, in 1946, was appointed Director of Housing for Westminster. In the 1940s and 50s, Liverpool architectural graduates filled city architects' posts in Birmingham, Manchester, Newcastle upon Tyne and Southampton.
Jonathan Cadwallader

BELOW: Myrtle Gardens was part of a grand ten-year plan put forward by Keay in response to 1933's Ministry of Health Circular 1331, demanding that local authorities develop programmes for slum clearance. Typically, Liverpool's was one of the most ambitious, proposing the construction of 5,000 houses in the suburbs and 10,692 flats in the inner city. Myrtle Gardens (built 1937) had 344 flats in a group of brick-built, five-storey blocks of distinctive appearance, including balconies and circular staircases at the ends of each building. Some four acres of open space, including children's play areas, was included in the overall development. Inspired by continental European housing schemes like Vienna's huge Karl-Marx-Hof (1927-30), designed by Karl Ehn (1884-1957), Myrtle Gardens represented a conscious break with tradition and the city addressing its critical housing problems. War damage and neglect of maintenance led to demolition of several of the blocks, despite attempts at refurbishment in the1960s, but Barratt Urban Renewal (Northern) stepped in and converted the remainder into flats for sale, opening as Minster Court in 1983. With the closure of the nearby Crown Street goods depot and landscaping of the site as a park, the environmental problems that blighted Myrtle Gardens have largely disappeared.*Liverpool Public Record Office*

TOP: Alongside new building, the Corporation has always been involved in slum clearance; the land released was then sold to private developers under strict controls, or used directly for municipal housing. Initially, the prime targets were the courts, cellar dwellings and substandard housing. After World War 2, there was an urgent need to re-house the people whose 120,000 homes had been damaged or destroyed. One immediate solution was the erection of some 3,500 'temporary homes' or 'prefabs', the first going up in 1946. *Liverpool Public Record Office*

BOTTOM: In the mid-1950s, the council identified 88,000 unfit dwellings in districts such as Everton and Toxteth. Some were undoubtedly substandard, but others could have benefited from modernisation. However, an underlying council policy at the time involved breaking the sectarian divide by re-housing people in out-of-town estates on a first-come, first-served basis. Then, in the mid-1960s, another 78,000 dwellings were deemed unfit, leading to a further wave of mass demolition and replacement by high-rise tower blocks, or dispersal to the outer suburbs or new towns such as Skelmersdale. The first tower block, the ten-storey Coronation Court, was opened on the East Lancashire Road in 1953. Gradually, the numbers increased, and when Logan Towers opened on Athol Street, in 1966, it was the largest prefabricated building in the world. This view highlights the transition in Everton, its new tower blocks contrasting with the steep streets and their serried ranks of terraced housing, none of which escaped demolition. *Liverpool Public Record Office*

THIS PAGE: The staggering level of destruction, including some outstanding Georgian and Victorian properties, was filmed by Nick Broomfield in his early 1970s documentary *Who Cares?* Retrospectively, much of this activity is now seen as a tragic mistake. Further images of the transition were taken by local author, photographer and historian Freddy O'Connor who, as a youngster, recorded the destruction of his city.

TOP: Ironically, dozens of these replacement towers have now gone, some after just 20 years, to be replaced by low-rise semidetached houses, suburban in style and often arranged in groups surrounded by open space. Today, large parts of central Liverpool have been redeveloped in this manner; with a declining population and little work, especially for those with few skills, the demand for inner urban land is low. Few regret the passing of blocks such as Haigh, Canterbury and Crosbie Heights ('the Piggeries') on William Henry Street, which failed socially and structurally as maintenance standards declined, rendering them uninhabitable.

In September 1969, Havelock Street, probably the steepest street in Liverpool, was in the process of demolition. In the foreground is a gas lamp, while the graffiti proclaims, 'Vote Protestant.' The tower blocks themselves are now history. *Neil Cossons*

ABOVE: Despite the (apparently unlearned) lesson of earlier, unwarranted demolition, some perfectly sound Liverpool housing stock has recently been knocked down or currently awaits the bulldozers. In the 1990s, the Centre for Urban and Regional Studies devised a plan for 'housing market renewal'. The CURS argued that, in order to prevent further depopulation of old inner city areas, 400,000 houses across Northern England needed to be demolished to stimulate urban regeneration. To achieve this, 12 pathfinders were incorporated into the Government's 2002 Communities Plan; one of which, New Heartlands, has overseen the demolition of parts of Bootle and Edge Hill and will shortly bulldoze areas of Welsh-built housing in places like Dingle, where there is currently a campaign to save for posterity the house that Ringo Starr grew up in. To date, Pathfinder has managed to demolish four times more houses than it has actually built. These boarded-up houses, with their distinctive Welsh yellow brickwork, were photographed on Ducie Street, Prince's Park, in 2010. *Neil Cossons*

SOME VANISHED STREETSCAPES

Corn Street, Toxteth. *Cedric Greenwood*

Vauxhall Road area. *J. G. Parkinson, Online Transport Archive*

Steeply graded Paddington, scene of a fatal tram runaway in 1934. *Courtesy G. W. Price*

ABOVE: Byrom Street, looking towards Scotland Road. Bessie Braddock, the famous Liverpool MP, used to buy her hats from the Co-operative Society building on the left. *Pam Eaton*

BELOW: Everton Road. *H. B. Priestley, National Tramway Museum*

BELOW RIGHT: Commutation Row. All the pubs in this view, including *The Hare and Hounds* (left) and *The Legs of Man* (right) have been demolished. This was used as a peak-hour tram loading point until 1955. As the trams were withdrawn, most of the roads were resurfaced, leading to the disappearance of the once-familiar setts. *Brian Martin*

ABOVE: In areas close to the waterfront, there has been a reversal of the long-term decline in inner urban population. Old warehouses have been converted to apartments as part of a worldwide trend, usually among young professionals, for living close to revitalised downtown cultural and retail centres, which can be traced back to Ghirardelli Square, San Francisco in the 1960s and the Inner Harbor, Baltimore in the 1970s.

In Liverpool, the incentives sprang from the government's response to the Toxteth riots of 1981. The Merseyside Task Force, with Michael Heseltine as Minister for Merseyside, set in train initiatives such as the renovation of the Albert Dock complex and the Liverpool Garden Festival. Today, housing associations maintain many former council houses and there have been a number of successful cooperatives; most notable is the Eldonian Community Association which, over a period of 30 years and in the face of brutal opposition by the city council during its period of control by Militant, has taken charge of the Eldon Street area of Vauxhall, close to the ex-Tate & Lyle site, Stanley Dock and the Leeds and Liverpool Canal, and carefully managed the process of housing replacement by and for the local community.

Today, although Liverpool is still beset by the problems it has suffered for generations – lack of work, low incomes, poor quality housing and the social and environmental issues that result – there is evidence to show that innovation and experiment are beginning to pay off. In the words of one ex-Corpy tenant, 'At least when I ask for something to be done, Berrybridge (a housing association) are there the next day.' *Jonathan Cadwallader*

ABOVE AND ABOVE RIGHT: There have also been successful residential developments away from the waterfront, for example on Shaw Street. *Jonathan Cadwallader (left), Neil Cossons (right)*

WELFARE AND MEDICAL PROVISION

Today, many Liverpool hospitals (together with the University School of Tropical Medicine) enjoy an international reputation. Over the years, Liverpool-based doctors and physicians have achieved an impressive list of firsts: the recognition of 'lunacy' as an illness; opening a school for the blind; isolating contagious patients; wearing clean gowns for operations; sending women health visitors into the slums; using ether as an anaesthetic; employing purpose-built ambulances, using the first X-ray machine; launching pioneer welfare centres, tuberculosis campaigns and birth control centres.

As the city grew, philanthropists also built an infirmary, an asylum, a dispensary, a hospital for seamen and a fever hospital, sometimes with money derived from the slave trade. Always slow to react, it was only when threatened by epidemics that the town council reluctantly agreed to provide the land for the Northern and Southern Hospitals, with the building money coming from private subscriptions.

The original Northern (1834-1902) was located near the dockland slums around Great Howard Street. Its replacement (1902-79) was often named after its prime benefactor as the David Lewis Northern Hospital. From 1929-48, most hospitals were the responsibility of the council. *J. G. Parkinson, Online Transport Archive*

The large bulk of Southern Hospital, opened in 1872, occupied a large area in Hill Street and Caryl Street, and was dismissed at the time as 'harsh and unpleasant'. During World War 2, it became a 'stone frigate' named HMS *Wellesley* and was used by the Admiralty to train Merchant Navy gunners. It closed as the Royal Southern Hospital in 1979. *Clive Garner collection*

TOP: The workhouse (built 1771) on Brownlow Hill eventually housed 5,000 destitute people in segregated dormitories. This aerial view highlights the sheer size of the establishment and its close proximity to the university (north) and areas of old tightly-knit housing (west). The site was sold to the Catholic Church in 1930.
Photographer unknown

BOTTOM: Designed by Alfred Waterhouse, Liverpool Royal Infirmary (1890-1978) was one of the largest and most innovative hospitals in the country. It was the direct successor of an infirmary established on the site now occupied by St George's Hall in 1743, until this was replaced in 1823 by a new hospital and lunatic asylum on Brownlow Street which, in 1851, was renamed the Liverpool Royal Infirmary. In turn, this gave way to Waterhouse Buildings. Before finalising his designs, Waterhouse consulted widely, most notably with Florence Nightingale (1820-1910), who advocated large windows and good ventilation. The hospital also had a novel heating system with steam pipes, radiators and air circulation.

Since 1994, the buildings have been owned by the university. Their spectacular glazed brick interiors, which include a chapel, have been carefully restored.
Liverpool Public Record Office

LEFT: Several buildings were dedicated to the welfare of the seafaring community, including the Sailors' Home (1849-1973) which was designed by John Cunningham along the lines of an Elizabethan or Jacobean mansion. Financed by public subscription, its benefactors hoped that by providing sailors with clean, affordable accommodation, they could 'arrest them from corrupting influences' of the demon drink and other vices. This 1969 view shows the extraordinary interior which, to make inmates feel at home, resembled a ship's quarters with 'cabins' arranged around five galleries or 'decks', and cast-iron railings incorporating strong nautical images, including Neptune, his tridents and convincingly knotted net.
Neil Cossons

BELOW: Above the main entrance on Paradise Street was this multifaceted nautical sculpture.
Neil Cossons

CEMETERIES

ABOVE: As the population increased, established graveyards failed to cope. From 1829-98, a privately funded, interdenominational 'necropolis' existed at St James Walk, Everton (later occupied by Grant Gardens). Faced by growing public revulsion over lack of suitable burial sites, the Corporation opened an all-faiths cemetery on Walton Lane, Anfield in 1863, which is still in business today. The imposing entrance, with its sandstone clock tower, dominates this scene photographed on 25 September 1937.

Bellamy-roof car 507 was typical of an older generation of four-wheel trams, of which the last survivor was withdrawn in 1949. To serve the city's two football grounds, sidings were laid in Priory Road (right) and a long storage track on Walton Lane. *Liverpool City Engineers*

Liverpool's pre-eminence as a port ensured that it was an early innovator in the field of power supply. Although controlled by private companies, Liverpool's first large-scale public utility was the supply of coal gas, which was then used for lighting. Today's natural gas network continues a service which began in earnest when the Liverpool Gas Light Company established coal gasworks in Dale Street (1816-53), Eccles Street/Vauxhall Road (1829-1934) and Caryl Street (1847-1924).

From 1824, the competing Liverpool Oil Gas Company supplied high-quality gas made from whale oil until 1835, the year after the company became Liverpool New Gas & Coke, with new works in Athol Street (1834-1968). In 1847, this company erected a large holder at Grafton Street. Instead of maintaining duplicate mains systems, the two companies amalgamated as the Liverpool United Gaslight Company in 1848. Until 1873, most feedstock was cannel coal which came from Wigan via the Leeds & Liverpool Canal, which had three gasworks (Eccles Street, Athol Street and Linacre) built alongside it. The first works with rail connections was Wavertree (1856-1968), while by far the largest was Linacre (1867-1974).

This view of Garston gasworks (1895-1972) was probably taken in the late 1920s, when the spirally-guided gasholder (bottom left) was new. The big gasholder (four million cubic feet) built in 1891-3 and named *Aerial* still stands today. In 1941, it was penetrated by a parachute mine which did not explode. First operational in 1895, it produced entirely carburetted water gas, a controversial American technology. The 'CWG House' was the block to the top right of the large holder. Next came the horizontal retort house, to make coal gas, followed by the vertical retorts (top right). Retorts were the closed chambers in which coal was heated and a retort house was the building which shielded the retorts. In the 1950s, a huge, barrel-vaulted retort house loomed over Banks Road. *J. B. Horne, Liverpool Public Record Office*

Conversion to natural gas during the 1960s and 70s led to the demolition of gasworks, including even the modern high-pressure plant at Linacre, whose oil-based feedstock was delivered by pipeline until North Sea gas rendered the works redundant. The 13 remaining traditional gasholders range from mid-Victorian structures with cast iron guide columns at Grafton Street and Linacre to a low-pressure, waterless MAN (German engineering firm Maschinenfabrik Augsburg-Nürnberg) holder erected on the site of the former CLC Brunswick locomotive shed in the late 1960s. As all are not in daily use and none is strictly needed to support the modern gas network, they could disappear should heavy maintenance be required.

This aerial view shows Lister Drive Power Station with its four distinctive chimney stacks – Matthew, Mark, Luke and John. *Liverpool Public Records Office*

In 1896, the Corporation acquired the Liverpool Electric Supply Company which since 1883 had supplied power to a small central area. Two new generating stations, Pumpfields (now demolished) and Lister Drive, were opened in 1900. Although the latter lacked a supply of cooling water, it quickly outstripped Pumpfields, which had no rail access but benefited from water taken from the Leeds & Liverpool Canal. During the 1920s and 30s, Liverpool took over the supply of several of its neighbours, including Bootle. Although upgraded and modernised into the late 1920s, Lister Drive declined until given a new lease of life by the Clean Air Act; it was converted from steam to oil in 1963, connected to the National Grid and fitted with gas turbines. This ended the need for the former extensive coal sidings, seen in the foreground of the picture below and electrically operated for some 30 years. These connected with the L&NWR Bootle branch. Although now closed, some sections of the power station are still standing.

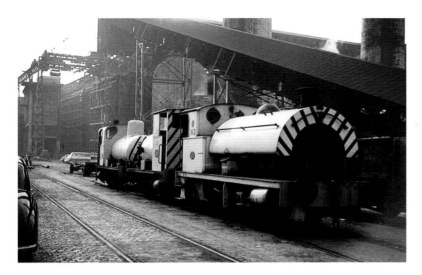

TOP: At various times, the Corporation's Electric Supply Department owned battery, electric, steam and fireless locomotives and, until the 1950s, a fleet of 20-ton hopper wagons. After the industry was nationalised in 1948, the locos were transferred to the Central Electricity Generating Board. Seen at Clarence Dock Power Station in 1964 are two fireless No 2 saddle tanks, products of Andrew Barclay. *B. D. Pyne, Online Transport Archive*

MIDDLE: Central government influenced the location of the Corporation's new 'super' generating station, opened in 1931 on the site of Clarence Dock as it was conveniently located for cooling water and deliveries of coal by water and rail. From the sidings (left), coal was despatched into the furnaces. First it was discharged by gravity into a silo from where it was then dropped onto a conveyor belt, supplying the bunkers. Expansion, modernisation and upgrading continued until the 1960s, by which time the station had 19 boilers, three boiler houses and three concrete chimneys which belched out smoke and were known locally as 'the three ugly sisters', or 'three wickets'. A connection to the National Grid was carried on gantries over the Leeds & Liverpool canal. The conversion to oil in 1963 led to significant job losses, the oil being pumped from Bramley-Moore Dock through a pipe running along the line of the former LOR into tanks in the stockade. Although closed in 1975, the station was not demolished until the late 1980s. *Courtesy Frederick Maxey*

BOTTOM: Within the stockyard (capacity 80,000 tons), which occupied part of the dock and was kept flooded to prevent spontaneous combustion, were three level luffing cranes for discharging and distributing the coal which came by rail from the Lancashire coalfields and by sea from Scotland, South Wales and, at times, the United States. Visible in the background are the tobacco warehouse, the two Stanley Dock warehouses (the one on the right badly damaged in the war, with the loss of over 130,000 tons of tobacco), the LOR at Clarence Dock station, a fireless locomotive (right) and Clarence Graving Docks (left). *Courtesy Frederick Maxey*

RELIGION AND CHURCHES

Today, the city's two contrasting cathedrals are potent reminders of the religious divide which played a major role in shaping its history, politics and culture. Until the mass arrivals of the Irish, Welsh and Scots, most people were reasonably tolerant of religious minorities, so that, by the end of the 18th century, there were churches and chapels representing most dominations – from Anglicans and Catholics to Quakers and Unitarians – and the small Jewish community had its first purpose-built synagogue on Seel Street.

However, even before the mass migration from Ireland in the 1840s, there had been periodic destructive violence by Protestants and Catholics, erupting from the former's demands for 'No Popery'. This intensified in the second half of the 19th century, as the population explosion placed a severe strain on the town's limited resources. Resentment ran deep, leading to ingrained bigotry, with many working-class parts of the city sharply divided on sectarian lines. Large numbers of Catholics and Protestants often co-existed in close proximity, with the former generally restricted to unskilled, poorly paid jobs in the docks, factories and warehouses, while the latter benefited from more skilled, better paid work. All too often, the hierarchy of both faiths was slow in demanding change.

Street violence erupted during Orange Day marches and charismatic street preachers railed against perceived threats. The sectarian divide distorted aspects of public life and influenced local politics, employment, housing and newspapers, with the police often caught in the middle and attacked by both sides. Many working-class Irish Catholics believed they were deliberately

Now a Unitarian chapel, one of the earliest centres of independent thought was the Ancient Chapel of Toxteth (built the early 1600s, rebuilt in 1774). Unitarianism is a movement to which Liverpool owes a great deal, as many of its liberal-thinking merchants, ship owners and businessmen were major benefactors, financing public works, cultural events, the university and, most importantly, charitable enterprises targeted at improving the lot of the poor. Unitarian 'domestic missions' attempted to break the poverty cycle by encouraging reading, writing and education.

Seen here in 1929, No 757, a short-lived experimental single-deck tram, passes the chapel on its approach to the Dingle. *W. A. Gilbert*

discriminated against, while many working-class Protestants (including the Ulster Irish) felt their way of life and their jobs were under threat from both Catholics and the Tory Anglican establishment.

This establishment was also opposed by the growing numbers of rural Welsh seeking a better life in Liverpool. As quarrymen they built the docks, engaged in trade and later built thousands of cheap, well-constructed houses, some of which remain today. They even had their own money (for seven years), regular *eisteddfodau* (cultural festivals) and many Welsh-speaking churches which became centres of non-conformist opposition to the Tory political leadership. As a result, the Welsh usually joined other non-conformists in voting Liberal while, in very general terms, Catholics tended to vote Irish Nationalist (or subsequently Labour, after creation of the Irish Free State in 1921) and Protestants voted Conservative. When the Tories won an election, the bells of St Nicholas's and St Peter's would peal out a blessing. A failed Fenian attack on the town hall led directly to the election of T. P. O'Connor as England's only Irish Nationalist MP, for the Scotland Division of Liverpool in 1885. A long-standing uneasy coalition between the Liberals and more liberally-minded Catholics splintered in the 1890s, with the Irish Nationalists becoming the dominant opposition on the city council. Some of the worst sectarian excesses occurred during the first part of the new century and, in a new twist, race riots occurred in 1919.

After World War 1 there was an overall diminution in sectarian violence but it still persisted into the 1950s, with some people asking are you 'pie' (protestant) or 'cake' (catholic)? It was the post-war plan to re-house people on a 'first come, first served' basis and not according to religious belief that finally broke the destructive sectarian strongholds. As old religious communities disappeared and church attendance declined, so ever more churches were closed. Today, it is difficult to understand the fear and prejudice which once ruled key parts of the city.

Many once-prominent churches vanished years ago. The parish church of St Peter's (1704-1922), later the Protestant cathedral and a cornerstone of Tory Anglicanism, probably housed the town's first public library and for many years hosted sacred music festivals. *Clive Garner collection*

ABOVE: As can be seen in this 1893 view, St Peter's was in prime position on Church Street. When it was marked for demolition, even Harrods prepared plans for a Liverpool branch to be built here, but in the event it was occupied in 1923 by a new Woolworth's. Beyond the church is the French-style T.R. Russell building and, in the distance, the façade of Central Station. *Francis Frith, Martin Jenkins, David Packer, Jerome McWatt, Online Transport Archive*

RIGHT: A rare glimpse of the steeple of St George's (1734-1900), built by Thomas Steers on the site of Liverpool Castle, the last remnants of which were removed in the early 1700s. When Lord Street was widened in the late 1820s and redesigned by John Foster Junior, substantial residential and commercial premises were built on the south side (left), all of which were subsequently destroyed in 1941. *Martin Jenkins collection, Online Transport Archive*

LEFT: After being reduced to a shell in 1941, the Corporation church of St Luke's (built in 1828), designed by John Foster Junior, was retained to remind future generations of the destruction suffered by the city during World War 2. *J. E. Marsh*

BELOW: Two St James in one: in 1948, the Anglican Cathedral seems to dwarf the older, Norman-style St James's Church (built 1775). Intended as the focal point for a new upmarket area, it makes early use of cast-iron columns to support interior galleries. Today the trams are gone and the church is no longer in use. *N. N. Forbes*

TOP: St George's (1813-1814) on Heyworth Street, Everton is one of two innovative cast-iron churches in the city, the other being St Michael's Aigburth. St George's is the product of collaboration between Thomas Rickman (1776-1841) and J. M. Gandy and was built by John Cragg (1767-1854), proprietor of the Mersey Iron Foundry. It is the first building with a completely cast-iron interior, a breathtakingly light confection based entirely on the use of slender and delicate cast columns and tracery. It exemplifies the enthusiasm of Cragg, a fanatic for cast iron, and his belief in its widespread application in buildings. Liverpool became a centre for the manufacture of prefabricated cast-iron buildings (some were even exported in kit form) and there were waterfront foundries that specialised in the work. The 'cast iron shore' as a metaphor for the Mersey derives from this. *Neil Cossons*

RIGHT: The celebrated architect E. W. Pugin (1834-75) designed several Catholic churches. Although listed, Our Lady Immaculate on St Domingo Road (built 1856) was demolished in the 1980s. It was conceived as an intended chapel for the new Catholic cathedral, which at one point was to have been built on this site. *A. S. Clayton, Online Transport Archive*

THE ANGLICAN CATHEDRAL

In sandstone grandeur on St James Mount stands Liverpool's great Anglican Cathedral, the climactic zenith of the long European tradition of Gothic cathedral building. The largest in Britain, its construction became the life's work of its architect, Sir Giles Gilbert Scott (1880-1960). Work started in 1904, at the peak of Liverpool's wealth and prosperity, in part to emphasise the Protestant ascendancy in a city with one of the largest Catholic populations in the country. Its completion, in 1978, coincided with the depths of the city's decline in the post-war years. The building's immensity is further amplified by the deep quarry nearby, which had provided much of the stone for the town's 18th-century buildings. It is now a disused cemetery containing the tomb of William Huskisson (1770-1830), killed by *Rocket* on the opening day of the Liverpool and Manchester Railway.

Scott was only 22 when he was appointed joint architect of St James's in 1903; he became sole architect from 1907. Extraordinarily, in 1909 he decided to redesign the whole building and, although construction of the foundations was well advanced, he replaced the original twin-tower design with the present massive single central tower. The refinement of the design and completion of the cathedral continued to occupy him until his death; although a Roman Catholic, he was buried outside *his* cathedral in 1960. Throughout the years of construction, work had continued even during the darkest days of World War 2, when part of the building was damaged. The tower was completed in 1942 and the cathedral in 1978.

The cathedral appears in a number of views in this book and at various stages of its construction. Today, the completed cathedral, with its massive 347-foot tower, is the one building above all others that dominates the city's skyline. The early 19th-century housing which once packed the slope down to Great George Street was cleared away and replaced in the 1980s by courts of three-storey houses. Inside the cathedral is a K2 telephone box, also designed by Gilbert Scott (in 1935) and still in commission. *Stephen Riley*

THE METROPOLITAN CATHEDRAL

Liverpool's Metropolitan Cathedral originated from similar motives to those that gave rise to its Anglican forebear at the other end of Hope Street. The commanding site at the top of Mount Pleasant, formerly occupied by the workhouse, was acquired in 1930, and Edwin Lutyens (1869-1944) was commissioned without competition to prepare designs for 'a cathedral in our time'. The result, a gigantic Romanesque composition, was to be bigger in every respect than its Anglican neighbour and larger than St Peter's in Rome; the top of the dome, at 510 feet, would dwarf the tower of the Anglican Cathedral. Building started in 1933 but, by the end of World War 2, with only the crypt complete, it became clear that the project's size was making it unaffordable and a competition for a new design was launched in 1959. The new building was to incorporate the Lutyens crypt and accommodate a congregation of 3,000 (later reduced to 2,000).

TOP: This view shows the present cathedral under construction in July 1965. Designed by Frederick Gibberd (1908-84), the circular structure based on 16 reinforced concrete trusses rises to a ring beam that supports the glazed lantern tower. The circular design reflected liturgical thinking at the time, with a central altar in sight of the whole congregation. *B. D. Pyne, Online Transport Archive*

RIGHT: The building was completed in just six years at a cost of £1.9 million and consecrated in 1967. Owing to its superficial resemblance to a tepee, it was swiftly nicknamed 'Paddy's Wigwam' or the 'Mersey Funnel'. Use of new and untried materials led to leaks and other damage and a major repair programme took place in the 1990s, somewhat altering the appearance of the Gibberd design. *Neil Cossons*

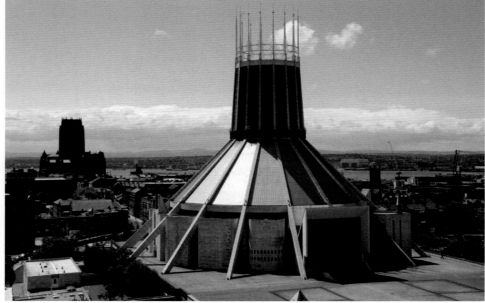

ABOVE: Liverpool has produced its share of fine journalists, many of whom cut their teeth with the *Daily Post* and the *Liverpool Echo*. First published in 1855 by a former chief constable, M. J. Whitty, the Daily Post cost only 1d. This was done deliberately to undercut the *Liverpool Mercury*, with which it merged in 1904. Founded by Alexander Jeans, the *Echo* was first published in 1879 from new premises on Victoria Street which it shared with the *Daily Post*. Until 1917, the *Echo* cost just a ½d. Both papers enjoyed wide circulations, stretching as far as the North Wales coast. On Saturdays, a special 'pink *Echo*' covered sporting fixtures. Over the decades, journalists have covered every aspect of the city's turbulent history and its photographers have taken a wealth of evocative images. *J. E. Marsh*

ABOVE: The old offices on Victoria Street had seemed very much at the heart of things, close to the theatres, pubs and markets. However, in 1973 they were vacated for new premises on Old Hall Street. Designed by Farmer & Dark, these have elevated walkways which formed an integral part of the 1965 plans for the central area. The papers became tabloids in the 1980s and today form part of the Trinity Mirror Group. *A. S. Clayton, Online Transport Archive*

XIII LAW AND ORDER

Relations between the police and some sections of the community have always been strained, ever since M. J. Whitty was appointed as the first chief constable in 1836. Sectarian areas were virtually self-policing, with both sides distrusting 'scuffers' and 'rozzers', viewing them as the enemy. Resentment permeated the waterfront where the law was seen as a tool of the employers, accused of breaking up strikes and lockouts. The legacy of police action in the transport strike of 1911 also left its mark. Conceived as a national strike against unemployment, it involved seamen, dockworkers and railwaymen, as well as municipal and tramway workers, although some of the latter were opposed to both the strike and union membership.

In August 1919, the police went on strike over pay and living conditions; their absence fuelled rioting, looting and burning, with major damage in Scotland Road and London Road. This time, HMS *Valiant* and two destroyers were despatched from Scapa Flow and no striking policeman was reinstated. Subsequently, Liverpool police were the first to have rubber-soled boots for night work, two-way radio communication and, in 1964, closed circuit television to detect crime. In the 1960s, the popular TV police series *Z Cars* was set on Merseyside. In 1981, the force was very much in the spotlight during the explosive Toxteth race riots. Today, Merseyside Police is divided into Basic Command Units with 11 police stations covering Liverpool itself. Relations with some communities remain tense.

Two days after the rally shown taking place here on St George's Hall plateau, crowds listening to the Liverpool strike leader Thomas Mann were dispersed by a police baton charge. In the ensuing violence, a policeman was killed, hundreds were injured, many arrested and old scores were settled during sectarian flare-ups in Great Homer Street and Islington Square. Fearing revolution, 3,000 troops were sent to the city and HMS *Antrim* sailed into the Mersey. On 15 August, soldiers escorting convicted strikers to Walton Gaol shot two people in the crowd. *Liverpool Fire Brigade*

Liverpool was the first UK city to have a salvage corps, formed in 1842, who worked closely with the fire brigade to minimise damage, especially to warehouse contents, as a result of fire or water damage. London followed suit in 1865 and Glasgow in 1873. The Liverpool corps was closed in 1984, as the fire brigade by then carried out such duties.

LEFT: Established in 1886, Liverpool has the oldest mounted police section in the country, based today in Allerton. This shot was taken during the 1968 Grand National.
J. G. Parkinson, Online Transport Archive

BELOW: Forming part of the police force since the 1830s, fire brigade members were known locally as 'fire bobbies'. After being absorbed into the new National Fire Service in 1941, the brigade became independent with its own chief officer in 1947. Posing outside the Jacobean-style main fire station on Hatton Garden (1898-2002) are ranks of fire bobbies with their engines. In earlier times, horse-drawn engines with steam-powered pumps had careered through the crowded streets at alarming speeds. Today, the HQ of the Merseyside County Fire Brigade is in Bootle.
Merseyside Fire Brigade

BELOW LEFT: Today, the main gaol is at Walton, although several early houses of correction still survive: The classic Main Bridewell (built late 1850s), designed by John Weightman as part of complex including a magistrates' court, still stands on Cheapside.
Jonathan Cadwallader

BELOW RIGHT: Two small lockups survive at Everton and Wavertree. This is the former (built 1787), a relic from the days when Everton was an independent village.
Neil Cossons

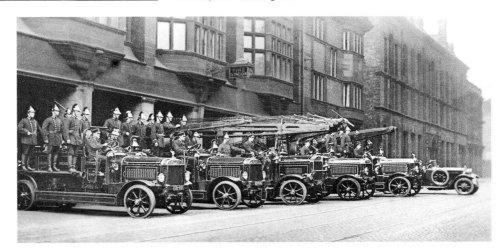

XIV LOCAL COMMERCE

Essential ingredients for overall well-being include plentiful supplies of fresh fruit, vegetables, meat and fish. In 1786, Liverpool City Council designated selected squares and streets for use as public markets, followed by a range of tolls in 1819. Of the 16 Corporation markets that remained in 1945, some operated in temporary premises following the bombing of the fish market (1873-1940) on Great Charlotte Street, St Martin's (Paddy's) Market (1826-1940) on Scotland Road and the wholesale fruit and vegetable markets (1840-1941) on Prescot Road, although Stanley abattoir and St John's Market (1822-1964) on Elliot Street also survived.

Although most suburbs had their own range of local shops, for decades those centred around Bold, Church, Elliot and Parker Streets, or in and around London Road, drew shoppers from a wide catchment area and played a vital role in sustaining the city's commercial prosperity. Today, many of the once highly individual stores have given way to the multinational chains which dominate St John's Precinct, Clayton Square Shopping Centre and Liverpool One. Church Street has been pedestrianised.

Built to designs by John Foster Junior, St John's Market's covered area was equal in size to St George's Hall, its wooden roof supported by iron pillars in some aspects a forerunner of subsequent train-sheds. It was close to the fish market and to Queen Square, another centre of local commerce. According to one newspaper report, market traders in this temple to what it described as 'God's Belly' sold everything from 'the unchristian black pudding to rat traps'. After closure, the vast complex was demolished to make way for St John's Centre (built 1970). Beneath its 450-foot high beacon is a modern market with over 200 stalls on two levels. *A. S. Clayton, Online Transport Archive*

TOP: Among the stalls in the surrounding narrow streets was a popular dog market, selling mostly puppies, on Market Street. In this mid-1930s scene, the McCormick's van is delivering poultry directly into the market (right).
John Collingwood collection

LEFT: This view of 'Holy Corner', the junction of Whitechapel with Church, Lord and Paradise Streets, was taken in 1908. In the background is Church Street, then one of the wealthiest streets in England. For 100 years it was the shopper's Mecca, dominated by names like Bon Marche, Coopers, Henderson's, George Henry Lees, C&A, Modes, Woolworth (the first branch to be opened in the UK, 1909), Marks & Spencer, Wynn's and Littlewoods. Within walking distance were Boodle & Dunthorne, Philip Son & Nephew, Watson Prickard, Owen Owen, St John's Market, Blackler's and Lewis's, as well as most major theatres, cinemas, hotels, cafés and restaurants.
Liverpool City Engineers

TOP: Founded in 1856 by David Lewis to provide clothes for ordinary people, Lewis's swiftly became the biggest store in the North, selling goods at competitive prices and introducing centralised buying. Its expansionist policies later included purchase of Selfridge's in London in the early 1950s. This Lewis's building (built 1910-13 and designed by G. de C. Fraser) was damaged during the war and replaced by the present building. In front is the Central Station Restaurant and W.H. Smith's bookstall. One of the most famous 'local' stores, Lewis's closed in 2010. *Clive Garner collection*

RIGHT: Rushworth & Dreaper's on Islington is greatly missed. Demolished for road building in 1960, it sold everything to do with music as well as supporting the 200-seater Rushworth Hall (the setting for many recitals), a lecture hall, a club room, a studio with a three-manual pipe organ and restaurant. *Clive Garner collection*

ENTERTAINMENT AND CULTURE XV

In the city's earliest times, the public flocked to spectacles such as cockfighting, bear and bull baiting and bare-knuckle fights; however, the emerging middle class sought greater edification. In the 1740s, Thomas Steers built a tiny theatre which was swiftly superseded by larger premises on the aptly named Drury Lane. However, it was the impressive *Theatre Royal* (built 1764) in Williamson Square that put Liverpool on the cultural map. Other theatres followed; some were outlets for 'high-class variety' or music hall, both of which suffered from the rise of cinema which forced closures or conversions. One of the last outposts of traditional variety was *The Rotunda* on Scotland Road, bombed in 1940.

Liverpool has a history of high-capacity venues for circuses, equestrian events, water shows, variety, pantomime, concerts, boxing, wrestling, plays and grand opera. Audiences could be boisterous, drunk and rowdy, especially on the cheaper tiered ranks of benches. Among these large auditoria were the *Royal Amphitheatre of Arts* (Great Charlotte Street, capacity 4,000, built 1826), the *Royal Coliseum* (Paradise Street, 3,000, 1856), *Hengler's Circus* (West Derby Road, 4,500, 1876), the *Royal Hippodrome* (West Derby Road, 4,000, 1902) and the *Olympia* (West Derby Road, 3,750, 1905). Only the latter is still in business, but the *Echo Arena* continues the tradition.

Still at the heart of its cultural life, the city's remaining theatres encountered severe financial problems during

For some 200 years, the *Theatre Royal* dominated the north side of Williamson Square. Designed by William Chambers, the building was enlarged in 1803 to include a semicircular stone frontage adorned with the Royal Coat of Arms. Great artists that performed here included Paganini, Franz Liszt, Edmund Kean, Julius Brutus Booth, Charles McCready, Charles Dickens, Sarah Siddons and John Philip Kemble, although the last two were seemingly hissed off the stage. The boy celebrity Master William Henry Betty, or 'Young Roscius', caused outbreaks of mass hysteria in 1804. Following financial difficulties and a short spell as a circus, the *Theatre Royal* closed in 1885 but survived as a cold storage depot until demolished in 1965, after efforts to save the Georgian façade had failed. *A. S. Clayton, Online Transport Archive*

the 1970s and 80s, some being threatened with closure and demolition. Today, the *Everyman*, *Playhouse*, *Royal Court*, *Empire* and *Neptune* seem to have secure futures; some are Listed buildings.

For many decades, cinemas were an essential part of the city's social fabric. Replacing music hall and variety as the prime source of cheap entertainment, there were some 90 central and suburban cinemas by the 1920s, many later absorbed by powerful circuits such as Associated British Cinemas, Gaumont British, Odeon and Paramount. A new generation of super cinemas were built between 1927-39, some with restaurants and cafés. Just as cinema killed music hall, so TV did the same for many cinemas. Most flourished into the 1950s by offering good value for money, although a few did end up as 'fleapits'. Before 'the big picture', audiences enjoyed a B-movie, a newsreel and sometimes a cartoon or a short; for children, Saturday matinees provided an exciting, noisy start to the weekend.

In the city, there were a couple of news theatres presenting rolling programmes of news, shorts and cartoons. Innovations such as colour, cinemascope and 3D failed to stop a spiral of closures during the 1950s-1970s; there are only a handful of cinemas left, of which the multi-screen *Odeon* (formerly the *Paramount*) has recently closed.

Over the years, Liverpool has produced many internationally renowned musicians including bands, groups, solo performers, conductors, instrumentalists and opera singers. From the mid-18th century onwards, festivals of sacred music were held in churches and assembly halls; concerts and recitals were later given in venues such as Picton and St George's Halls. Operas, operettas, ballets and minstrel shows featured at the *Theatre Royal*, the *Royal Amphitheatre*, the *Bold Street Music Hall* and *Queens Hall* (later *Queens Operetta House* and the *Bijou Opera House*).

Music has featured in the city's many pubs and clubs, some of which nurtured musical legends such as The Beatles and The Spinners in the 1960s, when the Mersey Beat became a worldwide phenomenon. Today, the city's venues cater for a range of musical tastes, with the 11,000-seat *Echo Arena* on King's Dock providing a reminder of earlier, high-capacity auditoria.

Occupying the east side of Williamson Square, the *Liverpool Playhouse* is the city's last functioning Victorian theatre. Designed by Edward Davies and opened in 1866 as the *New Star Music Hall*, it was home to the Liverpool Repertory Theatre Company from 1911-99, the oldest 'rep' in the country, whose roll call of stars and playwrights includes Michael Redgrave, Deryck Guyler, Noel Coward, Gertrude Lawrence, Rex Harrison, Anthony Hopkins, Cyril Luckham, Beryl Bainbridge, Richard Briers, Rita Tushingham, John Gregson, Derek Nimmo, Willy Russell and Alan Bleasdale. Structural alterations were made in 1895, 1969 and 2000; this view shows the 1969 extension (right) constructed around three cylinders. Since 1999, it has shared artistic management with the Everyman. *C. Squier, Online Transport Archive*

TOP: Historically, the present *Royal Court* (built 1938) occupies the site of John Cooke's *New Circus* (later the *Royal Amphitheatre*). Opened in 1826, it was close to the fish market (entrance visible to the right of the photograph) from whence 'fish stinks' pervaded the 4,000-seat auditorium. In 1881, it was redesigned as the *Royal Court Theatre and Opera House*, which was destroyed by fire in 1933. The designer of the present building, James Bushell Hutchins (1876-1953), incorporated several nautical themes. For years, '*the Court*' served as the city's No 1 venue for touring productions, especially West End plays and musicals, but as touring costs escalated so it faced closure and even demolition. Listed as Grade II since 1990, every effort is made today to conserve it as a live performance venue. *Clive Garner collection*

MIDDLE: Now part of the William Brown Street conservation area, this view illustrates the prime position occupied by the 2,400-seat *Empire Theatre* (built 1925) at the north end of Lime Street. The largest two-tier theatre in the country it was designed for Moss Empires by W. & T.R. Milburn and replaced an earlier theatre (1866-1924), which in turn replaced a spirits vault, a smithy and a coachworks. Owned today by the Empire Theatre (Merseyside) Trust Ltd, it has in recent years received a multimillion-pound facelift. Demolition of the Legs of Man public house (right) allowed for construction of an extension to the theatre. Over many years, audiences at this site have thrilled to legends such as Therese Tietjens, Marie Lloyd, Vesta Tilley, George Formby, Mae West, Bing Crosby, Frank Sinatra, The Beatles and Ken Dodd. The 132-foot Wellington Column (built 1863 and designed by George Anderson Lawson) stands on the site of Islington market. To the right of the column is Commutation Row, now gone, and beyond it the vast open spaces caused by the demolition of the 1960s and 70s. *G. Davies, Online Transport Archive*

LEFT: Author Martin Jenkins was closely involved in establishing the *Everyman* in 1964. It has a formidable reputation for new writing and encouraging young talent such as Jonathan Pryce, Julie Walters, Stephanie Beacham, Anthony Sher, Trevor Eve and Bill Nighy. After a decidedly rocky period, it is now linked artistically with the *Playhouse*. When this view was taken in 1961, the former chapel (built 1837) was the independent *Everyman Cinema*. *Pam Eaton*

TOP: One of the city's biggest theatres, the 4,000-seat *Royal Hippodrome Theatre* (1902) incorporated sections of *Hengler's Circus* (1876-1901) and led directly to construction of the nearby *Olympia*, another monster auditorium. When the Bellamy-roof tram was passing in 1905, '*the Hippo*' was staging twice-nightly music hall. After this regime ended in 1931 with Harry Champion and Vesta Tilley topping the final bill, it survived until 1970 as a 2,100-seat cinema. An increasing financial liability, the empty building was demolished in 1984.
The Cinema & Theatre Association

MIDDLE: Fortunately, the massive, Grade II-Listed *Olympia* remains as a mixed venue for performances, wrestling and even the occasional visiting circus.
Jonathan Cadwallader

BELOW: *The Astoria* on Walton Road was typical of those cinemas located on major transport arteries in the midst of large urban populations. The tram seen here was working its way into town from the Walton depot in 1955. *Pam Eaton*

BELOW RIGHT: To cater for larger audiences the 1,700-seat *Majestic* replaced on older building on the same site in 1937. Close to the major London Road/Moss Street junction, the attractive Gray & Evans design, with its eye-catching 75-foot tower, attracted local as well as city audiences by offering first releases at cheaper prices. Its policy of continuous showings from 1pm-11pm lasted until 1968. Following closure in 1970, it was demolished to make way for a new hospital.
Allan Clayton collection, Online Transport Archive

TOP: This late 1930s view has all four Lime Street cinemas in full swing. To the right of the Crosville Leyland Titan are the *Futurist* (1912-82) and *Scala* (1916-82), and to the left the *Forum* (1931-97) and *Palais de Luxe* (1906-59). The *Futurist* was the first purpose-built cinema in the city centre, whilst the '*Palais*' stood on the site of a much earlier entertainment centre featuring 'wonders' such as waxworks, dioramas and minstrel shows. When rebuilt in 1952 after a fire, the uninspiring façade featured sculptures of two film technicians. This site has now been redeveloped.
The Cinema & Theatre Association

MIDDLE: The *Rialto* was so damaged during the Toxteth riots that it had to be demolished. When it opened in 1927, the complex caused great excitement with its 1,700-seat cinema/theatre, magnificent ballroom, dozen shops, billiard room and café. The centrepiece of the Gray & Evans design was a colonnaded frontage flanked by two domed towers. Although patronage remained steady, especially for 3D and Cinemascope, after it closed in 1964 it became an antiques warehouse.
Clive Garner collection

LEFT: Financed privately by the Philharmonic Society, the first *Philharmonic Hall* (built 1849 and seen here) proved to be a first-class facility. Designed by John Cunningham (1799-1873), this well-appointed, two-storey, Italianate-style building drew audiences from a wide catchment area with its range of musical offerings. To the south stands the imposing Hope Street Unitarian chapel (now demolished). Following a catastrophic fire in 1933, its art deco-style replacement designed by Herbert Rowse was opened in 1939. Today, it is home to the Liverpool Philharmonic Orchestra. During the year, '*The Phil*' stages some 250 concerts including classical, rock and jazz, as well as films and solo gigs by performers such as Ken Dodd and Graham Norton.

XVI PUBS

From the 1820s, Liverpool earned a reputation for hard drinking as small breweries built rival alehouses to cater for the thirsty population. For many, drink provided an escape from poverty and drudgery, leading to drunkenness and domestic violence. Wages too were often paid in pubs and, although some responsible publicans did pass money to families, often it was swallowed before reaching the women and children.

By the 1860s there were 3000 drinking establishments concentrated around the docks, in the slums, near the town hall and the central market district. By the early 1920s, Bent's, Higson's, Threlfall's and Walker's Warrington Ales were predominant. Today, the only one of these still to have a presence in the city is Walker's (now part of Allied Breweries) and

scores of pubs have gone. Interwar slum clearance, wartime destruction, post-war re-housing, the running down of the docks, the loss of thousands of jobs and the advent of TV all hastened the decline of the pub culture.

ABOVE RIGHT: Among a hundred establishments within a quarter-mile of the town hall was *The Angel*, on the south side of Dale Street. Dating from the 1840s and demolished in 1962, it incorporated part of a former coaching inn, one of many pulled down to make room for Dale Street's grand new buildings. Standing on the corner of North John Street in the 1880s was the Royal Insurance Building (built 1845), later transformed into the more elaborate Head Office (1896-1903). *F. Frith, Martin Jenkins, David Packer and Jerome McWatt, Online Transport Archive*

RIGHT: The Vauxhall Road area near the docks once supported some 70 pubs, including the Castle on Tatlock Street, seen here in 1967. *A. S. Clayton, Online Transport Archive*

Many pubs in the vicinity of the city's long-gone central-area markets were once frequented by city traders, stall holders, porters, carters, businessmen, actors and 'Mary Ellens' (prostitutes).

TOP: Time has been called for the last time at the charming *Magic Clock* (formerly *The Champion*) on Roe Street. The cars are parked in Queen Square on the left. *Cedric Greenwood*

LEFT: The opportunity to pop in for a Double Diamond no longer applied at *The Old Dive* on the corner of Market Street. *A. S. Clayton, Online Transport Archive*

TOP: To slake the thirst of dock workers there were 40 or so competing pubs on the east side of Regent Road, including the *Palatine Hotel* (formerly the *Spirit Vaults*) on the corner with Dublin Street. *Cedric Greenwood*

MIDDLE: The area round Canning Place (known as Sailors Town) was notorious for drunkenness, debauchery, violence and press gangs. Here were wretched dosshouses and rooms for rent by the hour. Included in this group of now demolished buildings on Strand Street were older pubs such as *The Red Lion*, on the junction with Sea Brow. *Nigel Bowker*

RIGHT: The last Strand Street pub to close was *The Trawler*. Formerly *The Oceanic*, it was renamed after the loss of the *Titanic*. *Nigel Bowker*

Today football is big business, with its controversial club owners, high-earning managers and players. For decades though, it was a 'working-class sport' with 'working-class heroes' which attracted thousands to Goodison Park, home of Everton FC ('the Toffees') and Anfield, home of Liverpool FC ('the Reds'). In 'the 'Pool', football passions run high. Being an Everton or Liverpool supporter tends to take precedence over ethnic, religious or political divisions.

Interestingly, both teams emerged from the St Domingo Methodist Church Everton youth team. Founded in 1878, the team played at Anfield but, following an acrimonious split in 1892, some of the team established a new Everton ground a short distance away at Goodison Park, while the original ground became home to the newly-named Liverpool FC. Both teams have produced great managers, outstanding players (with Everton centre-forward 'Dixie' Dean as probably the greatest of all) and enjoyed national and international success. For the record, Anfield, which had the first goal-nets in the country in 1890, was also the venue for the first ever *Match of the Day* (broadcast 1965) and the first colour transmission (1969), while Goodison was the first to install electric snow-clearing equipment and the first to have programmes with team listings.

Although mainly associated with football, crowds do flock to Liverpool for other sports. The Grand National, the most famous steeplechase in the world, attracts large numbers. Over the years, punters have arrived on special trains from around the country as well by local trains,

Before the introduction of all-seated accommodation, Goodison, one of the largest and best equipped grounds in the country, could accommodate 80,000 as opposed to 63,000 at Anfield. Gone are the days when packed crowds swayed on the terraces, youngsters were passed to the front and a pee was taken through a rolled-up pink *Echo*. In the days before cars, transport links were vital for moving the huge crowds. Scores of trams and buses were provided, alongside some football special services. In 1956, crowds leaving Goodison surround the trams on Walton Lane.
Brian Martin

trams and buses. During the early 1960s, the course was threatened by redevelopment and two of four railway stations closed, including Aintree Racecourse which only opened on race days.

After several lean years, interest in 'the National' was reignited by the success of Red Rum during the 1970s. Today, huge crowds still arrive by road and rail and a few special excursions still operate.

Liverpool also has facilities for yachting, cricket, rugby, hockey, athletics and golf. Surprisingly, dockers once participated in amateur golf competitions against other ports. Boxing has thrived since bare-knuckle fighting became a potential route out of poverty. Some recent champions – such as Neil Tarleton, Pat McAteer, John Conteh and Alan Rudkin – built their reputations at the Liverpool Stadium in Bixteth Street. The most controversial sport today, hare coursing, continues at Altcar, where competition for the Waterloo Cup has taken place since 1836.

RIGHT: Floodlights were in use at Goodison Park from 1957 to 1972. *Tom Parkinson, Online Transport Archive*

BELOW: The gruelling 4½-mile course is designed to test both horse and rider as they tackle 'Beecher's', 'Valentine's', 'The Chair', 'The Canal Turn' and 'The 'Open Ditch'. In 1968 the race was won by Red Alligator at 100 to seven. Today, the race's future seems secure. *J. G. Parkinson, Online Transport Archive*

SELECT BIBLIOGRAPHY

Ackroyd, H., *Picture Palaces of Liverpool*, Bluecoat Press, 2002.

Anderson, P., *An Illustrated History of Liverpool's Railways*, Irwell Press, 1996.

Anon, *Bombers over Merseyside: The Authoritative History of the Blitz, 1940-41*, Scouse Press, 1983.

Belchem, J., *Irish, Catholic and Scouse*, Liverpool University Press, 2007.

Belchem, J., (ed.) *Liverpool 800: Culture, Character, History*, Liverpool University Press, 2006.

Butler, P., *Liverpool Airport: An Illustrated History*, Tempus, 2004.

Cadwallader, J. and Jenkins, M., *Merseyside Electrics*, Ian Allan Publishing, 2010.

Cavanagh, T., *Public Sculpture of Liverpool*, Liverpool University Press, 1997.

de Boufflers Taylor, S., *Two Centuries of Music in Liverpool*, Rockliff, 1970.

Dunne, J. & Richmond, P., *The World in One School: The History and Influence of the Liverpool School of Architecture 1894-2008*, Liverpool University Press, 2008.

Ferneyhough, F., *Liverpool and Manchester Railway: 1830-1980*, Robert Hale, 1980.

Gahan, J. W., *The Line Beneath the Liners: A Hundred Years of Mersey Railway Sights and Sounds*, Countywise, 1983.

Gahan, J. W., *Rails to Port and Starboard*, Countywise, 1992.

Gahan, J. W., *Seventeen Stations to Dingle: The Liverpool Overhead Railway Remembered*, Countywise, 1982.

Giles, C. and Hawkins, R., *Storehouses of Empire: Liverpool's Historic Warehouses*, English Heritage, 2004.

Greenwood, C., *Merseyside: The Indian Summer Volume One, Return to Woodside*, Silver Link Publishing, 2006.

Greenwood, C., *Merseyside: The Indian Summer Volume Two, Return to Pier Head*, Silver Link Publishing, 2007.

Hallam, W. B., *Fifty Years of Mersey Towage* (reprinted from *Sea Breezes*).

Horne, J. B. and Maund, T. B., *Liverpool Transport: 1830-1900 Volume One*, LRTA, 1975.

Horne, J. B. and Maund, T. B., *Liverpool Transport: 1900-1930 Volume Two*, LRTA, 1982.

Horne, J. B. and Maund, T. B., *Liverpool Transport: 1931-1939 Volume Three*, LRTA, 1987.

Horne, J. B. and Maund, T. B., *Liverpool Transport: 1939-1957 Volume Four*, LRTA, 1989.

Horne, J. B. and Maund, T. B., *Liverpool Transport: 1957-1986 Volume Five*, LRTA, 1991.

Hughes, Q., *Liverpool: City of Architecture*, Bluecoat Press, 1999.

Hughes, Q., *Seaport: Architecture and Townscape in Liverpool*, Lund Humphries, 1964.

Jarvis, A., *Liverpool Central Docks: An Illustrated History*, Alan Sutton; National Museums & Galleries on Merseyside, 1991.

Jarvis, A., *The Liverpool Dock Engineers*, Alan Sutton, 1996.

Jenkins, M. and Roberts, C., *Streets of Liverpool*, Ian Allan Publishing, 2007.

Joyce, J., *Roads, Rails and Ferries of Liverpool, 1900-1950*, Ian Allan Publishing, 1983.

Maund, T. B. and Jenkins, M., *Mersey Ferries Volume One: Woodside to Eastham*, Transport Publishing, 1991.

Maund, T. B. and Jenkins, M., *Mersey Ferries Volume Two: The Wallasey Ferries*, Black Dwarf, 2003.

McIntyre-Brown, A., *Liverpool: The First 1,000 Years*, Garlic Press, 2001.

McRonald, M., *The Irish Boats: Liverpool to Dublin Volume One*, Tempus, 2005.

Moss, W., *Georgian Liverpool: A Guide to the City in 1797*, Palatine, 2007.

Murray, N., *So Spirited a Town: Visions and Versions of Liverpool*, Liverpool University Press, 2007.

Pulson, D., (ed.) *My Liverpool: Famous Liverpudlians Talk About their City*, Tempus, 2000.

O'Connor, F., *A Pub on Every Corner, Volumes One-Four*, Bluecoat Press, 1995-2001.

O'Connor, F., *Liverpool: Our City, Our Heritage*, published by the author, 1990.

Rees, P., *A Guide to Merseyside's Industrial Past*, North Western Society for Industrial Archaeology; Countywise, 1984.

Sharples, J., *Liverpool*, Pevsner Architectural Guides; Yale, 2004.

Sharples, J., and Stonard, J., *Built on Commerce: Liverpool's Central Business District*, English Heritage, 2008.

Smith, P., (ed.) *Berlin Tempelhof, Liverpool Speke, Paris Le Bourget*, Caisse Nationale des Monuments et des Sites; Éditions du Patrimoine, 2000.

Stammers, M., *Mersey Flats and Flatmen*, Terence Dalton; National Museums & Galleries on Merseyside, 1993.

Welbourn, N., *Lost Lines: Liverpool and the Mersey*, Ian Allan Publishing, 2008.

Williams, P. H., *Liverpolitana: A Miscellany of People and Places*, Merseyside Civic Society, 1971.

Wright, G. F., *Mersey Docks Fleet List: 1850-1980*, Countywise, 2006.

A number of major dockland structures have been preserved, including the hydraulic power station at Toxteth Dock.
Jonathan Cadwallader